SCREEN ADAPTATIONS
CHARLES DICKENS'
GREAT EXPECTATIONS
THE RELATIONSHIP BETWEEN TEXT AND FILM

BRIAN MCFARLANE
EDITED BY IMELDA WHELEHAN

methuen | drama

To the memory of Valerie Hobson, a graceful Estella.

1 3 5 7 9 10 8 6 4 2

First published 2008

Methuen Drama
A & C Black Publishers Limited
38 Soho Square
London W1D 3HB
www.acblack.com
ISBN 978-0-7136-7909-0

A CIP catalogue record for this book is available
from the British Library

This book is produced using paper made from wood grown in
managed, sustainable forests. It is natural, renewable and
recyclable. The logging and manufacturing processes conform
to the environmental regulations of the country of origin.

Printed and bound in Great Britain by
CPI Cox & Wyman, Reading, Berkshire

contents

introduction

Dickens has been immensely popular with filmmakers, though it cannot be said that the resulting films have often been of major interest. Because he is, by common consent, a highly 'visual' writer, it may have been assumed that this means he is a gift to the cinema; this book will take issue with this on several grounds.

Sergei Eisenstein, the great Russian filmmaker, compared American film pioneer, D.W. Griffith to Dickens for 'their spontaneous childlike skill in story-telling'[1] and goes on to discuss Dickens as a forerunner of cinematic techniques such as the close-up. George Bluestone in one of the first studies of adaptation claimed that 'Griffith found in Dickens hints for every one of his major innovations'.[2] In my view the comparison has been too easily accepted, not sufficiently scrutinised. However, there is no denying the prolificacy of films derived from Dickens, and *Great Expectations* alone has attracted at least ten versions as well as several television

[1] Sergei Eisenstein, *Film Form*, ed. and trans. Jan Leyda, New York: Harcourt, Brace, 1949, p. 196.
[2] George Bluestone, *Novels into Film*, Berkeley and Los Angeles: University of California Press, 1957, p. 1.

adaptations. David Lean's 1946 film will be a major focus of this book: it has acquired an almost impregnable reputation and is generally held to be superior to Lean's version of *Oliver Twist* two years later. Both these contentions seem to me to be at least open to discussion.

The first recorded film adaptation appears to have been an American silent screen version in 1917, followed by a Danish silent in 1922, a US talkie in 1934, Lean's celebrated 1946 classic, the UK version of 1975 (made for TV but also widely shown in cinemas), an animated Australian film in 1980, and a modern reworking in the US-made adaptation of 1997. In addition, there have been at least five major television mini-series derived from the novel: in 1959, 1967, 1981, 1989, and 1999. There have also been many radio versions; at least three adaptations to the stage; an Australian mini-series, *Great Expectations: The Untold Story* (1986), which pursues Magwitch's antipodean adventures; at least three theatrical adaptations; and at least four novels inspired by aspects of Dickens's story; and a graphic novel version. I shall take up some of these other kinds of adaptation in the second chapter to emphasise the enduring appeal of this novel.

My aim in discussing the novel in the opening chapter is not to offer another, let alone definitive, reading of *Great Expectations*, but to consider some of the reasons for its continuing and wide-spread popularity and to explore some of the elements which one would need to have in mind when considering how it has been adapted, especially to the screen. Certainly, it is a novel which has had an unusual hold on the popular imagination. Later I will consider how two of the television serial versions have gone about their task; and will discuss the film versions made in 1934, 1975 and 1998 respectively. I have deliberately left Lean's 1946 film till the end, and have written it last. Having written about it at length before, I wanted to see how it stood up to comparison with the other, less well-known, less critically regarded versions, and to the passage of sixty years. Further, because the film has such a high critical standing, I wanted readers to have in mind, before reading about it at length, the other kinds of treatment the novel has attracted, without their simply being seen as cowering in the long shadow of the Lean film.

Great Expectations is one of those fictions which has taken on a longer and larger life than its maker can have envisaged. As recently as November 2006, objections were being raised to the Thames Gateway development partly on the grounds of violation of locations sanctified by Dickens having set part of *Great Expectations* there.[3] Indeed, one opposing voice claimed that the planned Thames Gateway would destroy, 'the old places where Magwitch tried to escape'. In the following month, playwright Patrick Marber talked of writing the screenplay for *Notes on a Scandal*, starring Judi Dench as a manipulative teacher, in these terms, claiming that he 'loves screen bitches': 'I remember seeing David Lean's *Great Expectations* when I was about 10. Miss Havisham and the cruel Estella always intrigued me. I was terrified. But one couldn't help wanting to have Estella be one's friend - as Pip did.'[4] And a recent Australian novel, Andrew McGahan's *White Earth* (2004), concerning the influences on a young boy's growth towards manhood, led one reviewer to conclude by saying: 'Those who have read Dickens will draw parallels between Uncle John and Miss Havisham and be aware of the Dickensian feel to both the progression of the tale and the overall tone'.[5]

[3] See *The Times*, 14 November 2006, for one account of the proposed development and the opposition to it.

[4] Quoted in Liz Hoggard, 'Far deadlier than the male', in *The Observer*, 3 December 2006.

[5] Sally Murphy, 'Book Review: *The White Earth*, by Andrew McGahan' (Melbourne: Allen & Unwin, 2004.) See www.aussiereviews.com/article1611.html

These three recent random examples suggest that *Great Expectations* is a novel whose afterlife is assured. Of the various adaptations that will be discussed in this book, one can only speculate on how long each will be remembered, but Patrick Marber's comment suggests that at least one – Lean's – is well on the way to having a place in the collective memory.

Acknowledgments

In helping me to obtain access to viewing copies of various film texts referred to in this study, I am indebted to Tom Burstall, who also answered many questions relating to his father Tim Burstall's television mini-series, *Great Expectations: The Untold Story*; and to Siobhan Dee and Helen Tully, respectively Collections Access and TV Acquisitions Officer at the National Film and Sound Archive, Melbourne. I thank David Field, Managing Director, Burbank Animation Studios Ltd, Sydney, who answered questions about the animated version of *Great Expectations*; and Trish Hayes, Archives Researcher, BBC, London, and Justine Sloan, of the Australian Broadcasting Commission's radio drama department, were extremely helpful about the extent of radio adaptations of the novel. On the matter of stage adaptations of *Great Expectations*, Jonathan Croall (London) and Monica Maughan (Melbourne) offered very useful first-hand impressions. I am grateful to my Monash University colleague, Dickens scholar Alan Dilnot for many helpful suggestions, and to Robert De Graauw for drawing my attention to the *South Park* episode which takes off from Dickens and to the graphic novel version of *Great Expectations*; to Terry Hayes, who brought Andrew McGahan's novel to my attention; to Ian Britain who put me on to Sue Roe's *Estella: Her Expectations*, and to Philippa Hawker for alerting me to Lloyd Jones's novel *Mr Pip* and for arranging with Text Publishing, Melbourne, to secure an advance copy for me. At the

British Film Institute, London, John Oliver, of the National Film and Television Archive, helped me considerably in researching various versions of the novel. To Oxford University Press, my thanks are due for permission to reproduce a table from my book *Novel Into Film: An Introduction to the Theory of Adaptation* (1996). I thank Imelda Whelehan, the editor associated with the production of this book and the staff of A&C Black Publishers.

And finally, my thanks are due to my wife Geraldine for all kinds of support during the writing, including a lot of valuably critical reading of the manuscript.

Brian McFarlane
Melbourne, December 2007

filmography and credits for key films

Television mini-series (page 52)
Great Expectations: The Untold Story (1986)

Director	Tim Burstall
Screenplay	Tim Burstall
Producer	Tom Burstall, Ray Alchin, for Australian Broadcasting Corporation (ABC), Hemdale Film Corporation, International Film Management
Photography	Peter Hendry
Costume design	Quentin Hole
Production design	Laurie Johnstone, John Pryce-Jones
Editing	Tony Kavanagh, Lyn Solly
Music	George Dreyfus

Running time 300 minutes (approx); also in a 102-minute tele-movie version

Main cast

Abel Magwitch	John Stanton
Tankerton	Ron Moody
Bridget Tankerton	Sigrid Thornton
Compeyson	Robert Coleby
Jaggers	Noel Ferrier
Pip (adult)	Todd Boyce
Pip (child)	Danny Simmonds
Estella	Anne Louise-Lambert
Miss Havisham	Julia Foster
Joe Gargery	Bruce Spence
Mrs Joe	Annie Byron
Wemmick	Alan Tobin
Herbert Pocket	David Sandford
Uncle Pumblechook	Brian Moll
Biddy	Nell Schofield
Molly	Jennifer Hagan
Sergeant	Tony (Anthony) Wager
Tooth	Gerard Kennedy

Television adaptations (page 65)

1981 mini-series

Director	Julian Amyes
Screenplay	James Andrew Hall
Producer	Barry Letts, for the BBC
Photography	John Kenway, Bob Hubbard
Costume design	Ann Arnold
Production design	Michael Edwards
Editing	Oliver White
Music	Paul Reade (composer/conductor)

Running time 290 minutes

Main cast

Pip (adult)	Jerry Sundquist
Pip (child)	Gordon McGrath (aged 8)
	Paul Davies-Prowles (aged 12)
Estella (adult)	Sarah-Jane Varley
Estella (child)	Patsy Kensit
Magwitch	Stratford Johns
Miss Havisham	Joan Hickson
Joe Gargery	Phillip Joseph
Mrs Joe	Marjorie Yates
Mr Jaggers	Derek Francis
Wemmick	Colin Jeavons
Herbert Pocket	Tim Munro
Uncle Pumblechook	John Stratton
Bentley Drummle	Iain Ormsby-Knox
Mr Pocket	Timothy Bateson
Biddy	Christine Absolom
Orlick	Lionel Haft
Molly	Julie Buckingham
Compeyson	Peter Whitbread
Aged P.	Tony Sympson

1999 mini-series (page 72)

Director	Julian Jarrold
Screenplay	Tony Marchant
Producer	David Snodin, for BBC and WGBH Boston
Photography	David Odd
Costume design	Odile Dicks-Mireaux
Production design	Alice Normington
Editing	Chris Gill
Music	Peter Salem

Running time 180 minutes

Main cast

Pip (adult)	Ioan Gruffudd
Pip (child)	Gabriel Thomson
Estella (adult)	Justine Waddell
Estella (child)	Gemma Gregory
Abel Magwitch	Bernard Hill
Miss Havisham	Charlotte Rampling
Joe Gargery	Clive Russell
Mrs Joe	Lesley Sharp
Mr Jaggers	Ian McDiarmid
Wemmick	Nicholas Woodeson
Herbert Pocket	Daniel Evans
Uncle Pumblechook	Terence Rigby
Bentley Drummle	James Hillier
Mr Pocket	David Horovitch
Biddy	Emma Cunniffe
Orlick	Tony Curran
Molly	Laila Morse
Compeyson	Donald Sumpter
Aged P.	Hugh Lloyd

Cinema films

1934 film (page 83)

Director	Stuart Walker
Screenplay	Gladys Unger
Producer	Stanley Bergerman, for Universal Pictures
Photography	George Robinson
Costume design	Vera West
Production design	Albert D'Agostino
Editing	Edward Curtiss
Music	Edward Ward

Running time 96 minutes

Main cast

Pip (adult)	Phillips Holmes
Pip (child)	George P. Breakston
Estella (adult)	Jane Wyatt
Estella (child)	Ann Howard
Abel Magwitch	Henry Hull
Miss Havisham	Florence Reed
Joe Gargery	Alan Hale
Mrs Joe	Rafaela Ottiano
Mr Jaggers	Francis L. Sullivan
Herbert Pocket	Walter Armitage
Uncle Pumblechook	Forrester Harvey
Bentley Drummle	Philip Dakin
Biddy	Valerie Hobson (scenes deleted)
Orlick	Harry Cording
Molly	Virginia Hammond
Compeyson	George Barraud

1975 film (page 95)

Director	Joseph Hardy
Screenplay	Sherman Yellen
Producer	Robert Fryer, for Incorporated Television Company (ITC) and Transcontinental Films
Photography	Freddie Young
Costume design	Elizabeth Haffenden, Joan Bridge
Production design	Terence Marsh
Editing	Bill Butler
Music	Maurice Jarre (composer/conductor)

Running time 124 minutes

Main cast

Pip (adult)	Michael York
Pip (child)	Simon Gipps-Kent
Estella	Sarah Miles
Abel Magwich	James Mason
Miss Havisham	Margaret Leighton
Joe Gargery	Joss Ackland
Mrs Joe	Rachel Roberts
Mr Jaggers	Anthony Quayle
Wemmick	Peter Bull
Herbert Pocket	Andrew Ray
Uncle Pumblechook	Robert Morley
Bentley Drummle	James Faulkner
Mr Pocket	David Horovitch
Biddy	Heather Sears
Molly	Celia Hewitt
Compeyson	Sam Kydd

1998 film (page 111)

Director	Alfonso Cuarón
Screenplay	Mitch Glazer
Producer	Art Linson, for 20th Century Fox
Photography	Emmanuel Lubezki
Costume design	Judianna Makovsky
Production Design	Tony Burrough
Editing	Steven Weisberg
Music	Patrick Doyle

Running time 111 minutes

Main cast

'Finn' Bell (adult)	Ethan Hawke
Finn (child)	Jeremy James Kissner
Estella (adult)	Gwyneth Paltrow
Estella (child)	Raquel Beaudene
Arthur Lustig	Robert De Niro
Nora Dinsmore	Anne Bancroft
Uncle Joe Coleman	Chris Cooper
Jerry Ragno	Josh Mostel
Maggie	Kim Dickens
Walter Plane	Hank Azaria
Lois Pope	Isabelle Anderson

1946 film (page 127)

Director	David Lean
Screenplay	David Lean, Ronald Neame, Anthony Havelock-Allan, with Kay Walsh und Cecil McGivern
Producer	Ronald Neame, (executive producer) Anthony Havelock-Allan, for Cineguild, Independent Producers
Photography	Guy Green (Robert Krasker opening sequences)
Costume design	Sophia Harris, with Margaret Furse
Production design	John Bryan, with Wilfred Shingleton
Editing	Jack Harris
Music	Walter Goehr (composer/conductor)

Running 118 minutes

Main cast

Pip (adult)	John Mills
Pip (child)	Anthony Wager
Estella (adult)	Valerie Hobson
Estella (child)	Jean Simmons
Abel Magwitch	Finlay Currie
Miss Havisham	Martita Hunt
Joe Gargery	Bernard Miles
Mrs Joe	Freda Jackson
Mr Jaggers	Francis L. Sullivan
Herbert Pocket (adult)	Alec Guinness
Herbert (child)	John Forrest
Wemmick	Ivor Barnard
Uncle Pumblechook	Hay Petrie
Bentley Drummle	Torin Thatcher
Biddy	Eileen Erskine
Molly	Valerie Hobson (uncredited)
Compeyson	George Hayes
Aged P.	O.B. Clarence
Sarah Pocket	Everley Gregg
Mr Wopsle	John Burch
Mrs Wopsle	Grace Denbigh-Russell
The sergeant	Richard George

Other films referred to

The Age of Innocence (1993) Directed by Martin Scorsese, for Cappa Productions.

The Barretts of Wimpole Street (1934) Directed by Sidney Franklin, for MGM.

Black Narcissus (1947) Directed by Michael Powell, for Archers Film Productions.

Bleak House (1921) Directed by Maurice Elvey, for Ideal Film Company.

Brief Encounter (1945) Directed by David Lean, for Cineguild, Independent Producers.

Brighton Rock (1947) Directed by John Boulting, for Charter Film Productions and Associated British Picture Corporation.

Cavalcade (1933) Directed by Frank Lloyd, for Fox Film Corporation.

Children of Men (2006) Directed by Alfonso Cuarón, for Universal Pictures, Strike Entertainment, Hit & Run Productions, Quietus Productions Ltd.

David Copperfield (1914) Directed by Thomas Bentley.

David Copperfield (1934) Directed by George Cukor, for MGM.

David Copperfield (1970) Directed by Delbert Mann, for Omnibus Productions.

Dr Zhivago (1965) Directed by David Lean, for MGM.

The Fallen Idol (1948) Directed by Carol Reed, for London Film Productions.

Frankenstein (1932) Directed by James Whale, for Universal Pictures.

Henry V (1944) Directed by Laurence Olivier, for Two Cities Films.

In Which We Serve (1942) Directed by Noël Coward and David Lean, for Two Cities Films.

The Invisible Man (1933) Directed by James Whale, for Universal Pictures.

Jane Eyre **(1971)** Directed by Delbert Mann, for Omnibus Productions.

Kidnapped **(1971)** Directed by Delbert Mann, for Omnibus Productions.

The Lady in the Lake **(1946)** Directed by Robert Montgomery, for Loew's Incorporated.

Lawrence of Arabia **(1962)** Directed by David Lean, for Horizon Pictures.

A Little Princess **(1995)** Directed by Alfonso Cuarón, for Baltimore Pictures and Warner Bros. Pictures.

Millions Like Us **(1943)** Directed by Frank Launder and Sidney Gilliat, for Gainsborough Pictures.

Mr Quilp **(1975)** Directed by Michael Tuchner, for Reader's Digest Films.

The Mystery of Edwin Drood **(1935)** Directed by Stuart Walker for Universal.

Notes on a Scandal **(2007)** Directed by Richard Eyre, for BBC Films, DNA Films, Scott Rudin Productions and UK Film Council.

Oliver! **(1968)** Directed by Carol Reed, for Romulus Films and Columbia Pictures Corporation.

Oliver Twist **(1948)** Directed by David Lean, for Cineguild, Independent Producers.

A Passage to India **(1982)** Directed by David Lean, for G.W. Films, John Heyman and Edward Sands.

The Passionate Friends **(1948)** Directed by David Lean, for Cineguild and Pinewood Films.

Random Harvest **(1942)** Directed by Mervyn LeRoy, for MGM.

Rebecca **(1940)** Directed by Alfred Hitchcock, for Selznick International Pictures.

Room at the Top **(1959)** Directed by Jack Clayton, for Remus Films.

Ryan's Daughter **(1970)** Directed by David Lean, for Faraway Productions.

Saturday Night and Sunday Morning **(1960)** Directed by Karel Reisz, for Woodfall Film Productions.

Scrooge **(1970)** Directed by Ronald Neame, for Waterbury Films.

A Tale of Two Cities **(1935)** Directed by Jack Conway, for MGM.

The Third Man **(1949)** Directed by Carol Reed, for London Film Productions.

This Happy Breed **(1944)** Directed by David Lean, for Cineguild and Two Cities.

The Way Ahead **(1944)** Directed by Carol Reed, for Two Cities Films.

The Wings of the Dove **(1947)** Directed by Iain Softley, for Miramax Films and Renaissance Films.

The Winslow Boy **(1948)** Directed by Anthony Asquith, for London Film Productions and British Lion Film Corporation.

Y tu mamá también **(2002)** Directed by Alfonso Cuarón, for Alianza Films International Inc., Anhelo Producciones, Besame Mucho Pictures and Producciones Anhelo.

PART 1:

Literary contexts

an enduringly popular novel

Why so?

Given the prolificacy of film and other versions, we must wonder at the perennial appeal of *Great Expectations*. There is at one level the attraction of the *Bildungsroman*: the novel that traces 'the development of the protagonist's mind and character, as he passes from childhood through varied experiences – and usually through a spiritual crisis – into maturity and the recognition of his identity and role in the world'.[1] Here we have the situation of a boy of humble origins who inherits a fortune which takes him away from those origins, leading him to become a snobbish spendthrift. Guiding our reading are such questions as: Will he eventually be redeemed? Will he be notably wiser at the end? That is, *Great Expectations'* essential plot turns on such universals of human experience as how we react to changes in our circumstances (for better, for worse or for both) and on the crucial element that chance may play in all our lives, and on how maturity will deal with us and we with it.

[1] M.H. Abrams, *A Glossary of Literary Terms* (4th edition). New York *et al*: Holt, Rinehart and Winston, 1981, p. 121.

This kind of novel includes such famous titles as *Sons and Lovers* and *A Portrait of the Artist as a Young Man*, but they haven't attracted anything like the same degree of interest from film-makers (or from fiction-makers in other media) as *Great Expectations* has. So, we may need to look further to understand what has drawn film-makers to this particular *Bildungsroman*. For one thing, the book also exhibits that sense of teeming life we associate with Dickens and the city. His evocation of London as a 'labyrinth' can, in Grahame Smith's words, 'create a response akin to that of leaving the cinema only to find the world outside flat and colourless.'[2] Perhaps the visual possibilities of the bulging, labyrinthine city, with contrasting returns to the marsh country of Pip's birth and childhood, invoking the binarism of village simplicities and metropolitan complexities as well as the continuities of cruelty, snobbery, affectation and benignity, help to explain film-makers' fascination with the novel. That is, this is also a novel preoccupied with matters of on-going significance, as well as with the specificities of time and place.

Though the phrase 'teeming life' is true of *Great Expectations*, in some ways the book is more single-minded, less complex than other works of Dickens's maturity such as *Our Mutual Friend* or *Bleak House*, without its having the fabulist austerity of *Hard Times*. Here the maturity is felt in the concentration on Pip as protagonist. There is a strong sense of Pip's being at the centre of pools of characters who attract the spotlight as and when they bear upon his changing fortunes, and they are chiefly important for that reason. This is not one of those Dickensian narratives in which sub-plots proliferate: we can forget Oliver himself in *Oliver Twist* for chapters at a time, while we try to work out Monks' tale or while we follow Bill Sikes' flight: here,

[2] Grahame Smith, *Dickens and the Dream of Cinema*. Manchester and New York: Manchester University Press, 2003, p. 63.

though, everything matters insofar as it bears on Pip. There is the usual large cast of entertaining grotesques, but they are significant for how they affect the course of Pip's life and are kept in their place by the firm hand of Dickens's thematic intentions.

How does it work?
Serial

The novel first appeared as a serial, running through thirty-six weekly instalments of the journal, *All the Year Round*, from December 1860 to August 1861, each issue running one or two chapters of the novel as it would be ultimately published in 1861. This serial publication, very common with nineteenth-century novels, had important implications for the structuring of the novel's narrative. Each instalment needed to have some sort of inner coherence: each required at least a minor sense of climax as well as leaving the reader with the tantalising prospect of the ensuing instalment to answer questions left hanging in the current one. If the novel was not to seem merely a string of more or less exciting events, the author clearly needed to have an over-all sense of the place of each episode in the scheme of the novel as a whole. In this way, the serial publication had its effect on structural matters. This is not to say anything new or complicated; simply that it is a fact that has to be taken into account when we consider how the book is put together. In matters of tone and atmosphere, the process of serialisation no doubt impressed on the author some need for variety not only between but, as well, *within* instalments.

Stages

Great Expectations is, as noted already, by Dickens's standards quite unusually single-minded as far as its narrative focus is concerned. Shorn of sub-plots, it concentrates our attention on Pip's story and everything in the novel bears on Pip, either because he is involved *in* events or because they reflect thematically on his development. Dickens seems to have intended this structural tightness (though that term does not imply a schematic organisation) by his division of the novel into three parts of almost exactly equal length and by his description of these parts as 'stages(s) of Pip's expectations'. The first stage (Chapters I–XIX) begins with Pip's childhood meeting in the gloomy churchyard with the convict Magwitch, includes his crucial meeting with the reclusive Miss Havisham and her ward Estella, and ends with his heading for London to take up the terms of his expectations: 'and the world lay spread before me'.[3] The second stage (Chapters XX–XXXIX) relates Pip's London life, his becoming a gentleman, and ends with the return of Magwitch who undermines Pip's pretensions by revealing himself as the source of Pip's expectations: 'and the wind and rain intensified the thick black darkness' (Ch. XXXIX). In the third and last stage, Pip must face the consequences of this knowledge, what it means in relation to his own future, to the possibility of his having been intended for Estella, and to his own moral growth: 'so, the mists were rising now … and I saw no shadow of another parting from her' (Ch. LIX).

This very brief summary of the 'action' of the three stages is intended to reinforce my point about the structural firmness and shapeliness of the novel, as well as to indicate the poetic insight that ends each stage with a comment on the physical world, while imbuing this with a profound psychological insight. This is at heart the story of a poor boy's being rewarded for an act he did out of fear rather than innate goodness of heart, of his being in some way

[3] *Great Expectations.* Thomas Nelson and Sons edition. Undated, probably c1960, p. 162 . Further references to the novel throughout this and subsequent chapters will be in the form of parenthetical chapter references in the main body of the text.

corrupted by this reward, and finally learning to make the kinds of moral discrimination by which we assume he will live the rest of his life. The first stage of the novel is rich in incident: startling in the graveyard encounter, grimly and wildly comic in episodes such as the Christmas dinner, and bizarre as in the visit to Satis House which introduces Pip to Estella, unrequited love for whom dominates his life over the next few years. In articulating a drama of psychological realism, as far as Pip's education is concerned, the novel nevertheless embraces the gothic in its presentation of Miss Havisham and Satis House, and of melodrama in the attack on Pip's shrewish sister, Mrs Joe Gargery, apparently with a convict's leg-iron. Generally though, this first stage is characterised by Pip's encountering those who will influence the rest of life as far as the novel reveals it.

The second stage is primarily concerned with Pip's London 'education' (academic as well as social) and with the mounting frustration of his infatuation with Estella, both of which strands are – though Pip doesn't fully realise it – brought to a head with the return of Magwitch. A centrally important scene in relation to Pip's development is that in which his simple, good-hearted brother-in-law Joe Gargery comes to visit him in London and inadvertently forces Pip to look inwards and not to care for the snobbish 'gentleman' he realises he has become. It is in the last stage that Pip, aware now of the slender basis of his aspirations, puts his own disappointed hopes to one side in an abortive effort to rescue Magwitch by spiriting him out of the reach of the law. As Magwitch, lying near to death in the prison infirmary, tells him, 'And what's best of all … you've been more comfortable alonger me, since I was under a dark cloud, than when the sun shone' (Ch. LVI). In the *Bildungsroman* mode, Pip has undergone a journey towards a wisdom of the heart that enables him not merely to do right by

Magwitch but to value what Joe has always stood for: a goodness that comes from always placing the needs of others before one's own selfish desires. As Frank Magill put it, writing of both Pip and David Copperfield, 'As he casts off his own weakness and better understands the dangers of the world, he succeeds – that is to say, he advances through the class system – and ends up less brash, a chastened but wiser man'.[4]

Cardinal functions

Roland Barthes has claimed that 'A narrative is never made up of anything other than functions: in differing degrees, everything signifies.'[5] He divides functions into two main groups: distributional and integrational. The former, to simplify, refers to actions and events which operate 'horizontally' in the narrative; the latter refers to 'a more or less diffuse concept which is nevertheless necessary to the meaning of the story',[6] including matters of character and atmosphere, and which operates 'vertically' in the narrative. It is to Barthes' idea of 'cardinal functions', the key distributional functions, that I want to draw attention to here. He goes on to say: 'Returning to the class of functions, its units are not all of the same "importance": some constitute real hinge-points of the narrative (or a fragment of the narrative) ... For a function to be cardinal, it is enough that the action to which it refers open (or continue, or close) an alternative that is of direct consequence for the subsequent development of the story'.[7] In the table below I have listed what seem to me to be

[4] Frank N. Magill (ed), *Cinema: The Novel Into Film*. Pasadena: Salem (1980) 1976 edition, p. 212.

[5] Roland Barthes, 'Introduction to the Structural Analysis of Narratives' (1966) in *Image-Music-Text*, trans. Stephen Heath. Glasgow: Fontana/Collins, 1977, p. 89.

[6] Ibid, p. 92.

[7] Ibid, pp. 93–94.

major cardinal functions in *Great Expectations,* major in the sense that without any one of them the outcome might have been different:[8]

1	Pip meets Magwitch in village churchyard.
2	Pip steals food and file for Magwitch.
3	Soldiers capture Magwitch and second convict, Compeyson.
4	Pip visits Satis House, meets Miss Havisham and Estella.
5	Stranger at inn gives Pip a shilling wrapped in two pound notes, and stirs grog with Joe's file.
6	Pip returns to Satis House, meets Mr Jaggers, and fights Herbert Pocket.
7	Pip visits Satis House again.
8	Miss Havisham gives Joe £25 for Pip's indentures as blacksmith's apprentice.
9	Joe takes on Orlick as journeyman worker in forge.
10	Pip re-visits Satis House. Estella has gone abroad.
11	Mrs Joe is brutally attacked (apparently with convict's leg-iron).
12	Biddy comes to live at the Gargery house.
13	Pip tells Biddy he wants to become a gentleman.
14	Jaggers brings news of Pip's 'great expectations'.
15	Pip goes to London.
16	He sets up house with Herbert Pocket at Barnard's Inn.
17	Herbert tells story of Miss Havisham's jilting.
18	Pip goes to Hammersmith, to be educated by Mr Pocket.
19	Pip gets money from Jaggers to set himself up.

[8] This table first appeared in Brian McFarlane, *Novel to Film: An Introduction to the Theory of Adaptation.* Oxford: Clarendon Press, 1996, pp. 113–115. It is reproduced here by permission of the Oxford University Press.

20	Pip dines with Jaggers (along with Herbert and Bentley Drummle).
21	Joe visits Pip at Barnard's Inn.
22	Pip visits Miss Havisham at her request (via Joe).
23	Pip re-meets Estella.
24	Pip secures Orlick's dismissal as gate-keeper at Satis House.
25	Pip and Herbert exchange their romantic secrets.
26	Pip meets and escorts Estella in London.
27	Pip and Herbert fall into debt.
28	Mrs Joe dies.
29	Pip returns to village for funeral.
30	Pip's income is fixed at £500 a year when he comes of age.
31	Pip takes Estella to Satis House.
32	She and Miss Havisham quarrel.
33	At Assembly Ball, Estella leads on Bentley Drummle.
34	Magwitch returns to reveal himself as Pip's benefactor.
35	Pip verifies Magwitch's story with Jaggers.
36	Pip and Herbert make plans for Magwitch's escape.
37	Magwitch tells story of his past (involving Miss Havisham and Compeyson).
38	Pip goes to farewell Miss Havisham and Estella.
39	Estella tells him she is to marry Drummle.
40	Wemmick warns Pip of being watched.
41	Pip, with help of Herbert and Wemmick, makes further plans for Magwitch's escape.
42	Pip visits Satis House to ask Miss Havisham to finance Herbert.
43	Pip tries to save Miss Havisham from burning.
44	Jaggers (reluctantly) tells Pip Estella's true story.
45	Pip goes to deserted sluice house.

46	Pip is saved from death at Orlick's hand by arrival of Herbert and others at sluice house.
47	The escape plan for Magwitch fails.
48	Pip loses fortune.
49	Magwitch is tried.
50	Magwitch dies in prison.
51	Pip becomes ill.
52	Joe looks after Pip.
53	Biddy and Joe get married.
54	Pip re-meets Estella in the ruins of Satis House.

Though it might be argued that there are other possible contenders for the 'cardinal function' label, I should still argue that all the above listed 'events' are crucial to the working out of the plot, in the sense that they all permit alternative outcomes. Remove any one of them and the course of the narrative might be different. Again, these cardinal functions are roughly divided among the three stages into which Dickens has divided his story.

What does it mean?

It is one thing to try to isolate the key events of the novel on the basis of those which govern the outcome of the story; it is another, and more important, to try to discern what kinds of patterns those events, and the characters participating in them, might reveal.

The Bildungsroman

As suggested above, you can interpret the events of the novel as falling within the parameters of what is understood by the German term, *Bildungsroman*, which, in the words of one definition 'deals with maturation, wherein the hero becomes "civilised" i.e., becomes aware of himself as he relates to the objective world outside his subjective consciousness.'[9] The term, first applied to Goethe's *Wilhelm Meister* (1795–96; translated into English in 1824), is helpful in relation to *Great Expectations* which can very reasonably be seen as a novel of 'formation' or 'education', as implied by the German word. The 'education' which 'forms' Pip is scarcely a formal one but is rather a matter of influences which shape his development, though he is certainly made aware of gaps in such education as he has had. One of the comic highlights of the account of Pip's early childhood is the description of 'The Educational Scheme or Course established by Mr Wopsle's great-aunt':

> The pupils ate apples and put straws down one another's backs, until Mr Wopsle's great-aunt collected her energies, and made an indiscriminate totter at them with a birch-rod. After receiving the charge with every mark of derision, the pupils formed in line and buzzingly passed a ragged book from hand to hand. The book had an alphabet, some figures and tables, and a little spelling – that is to say, it had had once. As soon as this volume began to circulate, Mr Wopsle's great-aunt fell into a state of coma ... (Ch. X).

Comic as this is, Dickens is here making a serious point for the purpose of his larger thematic preoccupation, as indeed, I would claim, everything in this novel does work towards its ultimate coherence. Pip, smitten by Estella's imperious charms, has divined that the way to improve himself is through learning more. Even before meeting Estella, he has answered Joe's 'What a scholar you are!' with 'I should like to be' (Ch. VII). He draws from Biddy all she

[9] Sylvan Barnet *et al*, *A Dictionary of Literary Terms*. London: Constable, 1964, pp. 100–101.

knows, which, in intellectual matters, is not much, and a little later he confides to her: 'I want to be a gentleman' (Ch. XVII), and, further, that he wants her to help Joe 'in his learning and his manners' (Ch. XIX). In the confused state of the young Pip's mind, he sees education and social advancement as intricately connected. When he knocks the 'pale young gentleman' down in the grounds of Satis House, he is in no doubt that Herbert *is* a gentleman, and he fears that 'village boys could not go stalking about the country, ravaging the houses of gentlefolks and pitching into the studious youth of England, without laying themselves open to severe punishment' (Ch. XII). It is his youthful notion of what constitutes a 'gentleman' that will have to undergo serious revision during the ensuing processes of his education; his perception of Herbert is not only that he is a gentleman but that he is 'studious' as well.

The course of Pip's education enters a more formal phase when he becomes one of Mr Matthew Pocket's students. Mr Pocket, despite having distinguished himself at Harrow and Cambridge, and despite – or because of – having married a lady of (absurd) social pretensions, has generally failed to make his mark in the world. 'Education' has not led to worldly success for him, but more important for Pip's development is the gentle demeanour he shares with Herbert, whose optimism in the face of limited prospects, and whose tactful intervention in the matter of London manners, are also truly valuable to Pip. We assume that part of Pip's education involves the acquisition of social graces; that is, those of the kind demonstrated by the meetings of The Finches of the Grove, the idiotic gentleman's club in which he comes up against Bentley Drummle, another of Mr Pocket's students, in an acrimonious way deriving from Drummle's toasting Estella.

Influences

What matters more is the way in which Pip grows as a result of the influences at work in his life, though there is no shame in his wishing to be better educated. There is not much hope for this in the village or local market town: Joe is gentle and loving and his goodness, and Pip's recognition of it, will be crucial to Pip's growth: he is not however in a position to teach anything in the way of *knowledge*, his own being limited to the forge. And those (very funny) caricatures who sit around the Christmas dinner table, prosing about 'Pork' as a subject for sermons or the ingratitude of the young, are ignorant, and unaware of how ignorant they are. Pip's two chief encounters in the first 'stage' are with Magwitch and with Miss Havisham and Estella, and they work in disparate ways on the boy's nascent understanding.

The alarming encounter with Magwitch intensifies that sense of guilt that is always being instilled in Pip by his virago sister who implies that the mere fact of his being born was an act of deliberate provocation. When Pip steals her pie and brandy for Magwitch, he feels he is being associated with the convict class, that class so likely to end on the gibbet which stands (both realistically and symbolically) on the marshes. The look and shake of the head that passes from Pip to the captured convict seems another connection of guilty complicity: 'I had been waiting for him to see me, that I might try to assure him of my innocence' (Ch. V): innocence, that is, of betraying the convict's whereabouts, not of the act of theft which he has carried out through fear. When Mrs Joe is later struck down by the file that had come wrapped round with two pound notes as a gift to Pip from Magwitch in Australia, Pip 'was at first disposed to believe that *I* must have had some hand in the attack upon my sister' (Ch. XVI). He has so often felt the harshness of her tongue and the energy of her thrashings that it is as though he has nurtured guilty fantasies of reprisal. As it happens, it is the journeyman Orlick who is the guilty one. All Pip's association with Magwitch at this stage feeds into his repugnance for the returned convict at the end of the novel's second stage.

The visit to Satis House has influences of a different kind, but no more conducive to tranquillity. The positive aspect of the meeting with the bizarre recluse, Miss Havisham, is in the way it fires his imagination. Even in its condition of musty desuetude, Satis House is like nothing Pip has ever seen before; nor does the idea of a woman who has never seen the sun since before he was born fit easily into the narrow parameters of his experience. When he returns to the forge and is badgered by Mrs Joe for details of the visit, his mendacious flights suggest that his imaginative faculties *have* been fired. And of course, at Satis House he meets Estella who becomes the romantic obsession of his life, though at this point she destroys his peace of mind by the class-based cruelty of her referring to him as 'a common labouring boy' (p. viii). The night after that first visit he reflects how common Estella would consider Joe, a mere blacksmith (Ch. IX); and later when Joe accompanies him to Satis House to receive the money for Pip's indentures, the narrating Pip records: 'I am afraid that I was ashamed of the dear good fellow – I *know* I was ashamed of him' (Ch. XIII) and his shame is intensified by noting that Estella's 'eyes laughed mischievously' at Joe's gaucherie. Joe, goodness itself, *is* embarrassing on this occasion: his shyness away from the forge and the marshes makes him seem foolish and deprives him of the simple dignity he can command in his own setting. 'It is a most miserable thing to feel ashamed of home' is the opening sentence of Chapter XIV in which Pip considers how the meeting with Estella has unsettled him for the life he has been used to.

In this most carefully, even subtly, constructed of Dickens's novels, it is the arrival of Jaggers with the news of Pip's expectations which brings together the two strands of influence – those exerted by Magwitch and by Satis House. It might be argued that there is something too contrived about this arrangement – Pip believing himself singled out for advancement by Miss Havisham, but in fact the beneficiary of a convict who has done well for himself – and perhaps in realist terms this is so. Christopher Ricks felt that 'It is more than a pity that the coincidences on which the plot depends (Jaggers being the lawyer of both Miss Havisham and Magwitch, and Magwitch being Estella's father) should not be revealed until almost the end of the novel ... (and) as a means of rounding it off'.[10] But there is more at stake here than an offence against 'realism': Jaggers' connection both with the source of Pip's good fortune and with the one he assumes – *wants* to believe – is his benefactor is a symbolic way of yoking together the guilt and shame that have so clouded the younger Pip's life and the extremes of class difference these two influences represent. In plot terms, Jaggers' announcement is the turning point: Magwitch will indeed affect in every way – and significantly *effect* – Pip's development; Miss Havisham will have no direct bearing on the plot, except, as noted, in widening Pip's imaginative grasp and in being the means of introducing Estella into his life.

Connections

Part of the textural richness of *Great Expectations* lies in the way its events and the characters involved in them embody the shifting connections between morality on the one hand and class and wealth on the other. Because these distinctions are worked out with

[10] Christopher Ricks, *'Great Expectations'* in J. Cross and G. Pearson (eds.) *Dickens in the Twentieth Century* (1962), reprinted in E. Rosenberg (ed) *Great Expectations*, A Norton Critical Anthology. London and New York: W.W. Norton, 1999, p. 673.

acute psychological and social realism the novel again avoids schematism. It is not, as *Hard Times* for better and worse is, allegorical in its representation of such abstractions; it is not a moral fable but a densely patterned novel in which the individual remains as much *that* as representational. It is not a matter of reading Pip's story as that of an innocent boy corrupted by unexpected fortune, stubbing his toe against the social system, and finishing a sadder but certainly wiser man.

Everywhere you look in the novel, you find such issues being enacted in its relationships, in the action that constitutes its plot. So, Joe is kind and true and, in the novel's 'agenda', that sort of virtue will be vindicated in the end. It is he who pays the debts of the newly bankrupted Pip; It is he who nurses him through the illness following his abortive attempt to save Magwitch. Nevertheless, the novel never for a moment suggests that Joe could have answered all the needs of the growing Pip. When Joe visits Pip in London, his innate goodness is no guarantee that he will not be to Pip the kind of embarrassment he had been on that earlier occasion at Satis House. The novel is wise enough to appreciate this: it allows the mature Pip to reflect on the snobbishness that has made him sensitive to Joe's gaucherie in Barnard's Inn, and wise enough to allow Joe to be aware of how awkward he is in London. Miss Havisham has considerable wealth at her disposal but there is no reliable connection between this and her treatment of others. She allows Pip to believe she may be his benefactor; she taunts her Pocket relations with the prospect of expectations; and above all she warps the ordinary human development of Estella into a chill agent of revenge on the male sex.

Class has raised its cruel head in Estella's early treatment of Pip. As already noted, she makes him ashamed of his origins and his home. The coincidence of her being Magwitch's daughter is then more than a plot device: it is Dickens's way of offering a critique of a class-based criterion of assessment, and this is further dramatised in the affectations of Mrs Pocket and Bentley Drummle. Mrs Pocket had been, with scant justification for such aspiration, 'brought up from the cradle as one who in the nature of things must marry a title' (Ch. XXIII), but has married Mr Pocket whose manifest virtues do not run to wealth or high social distinction. Drummle, on the other hand, is just two steps away from a title, persistently alludes to Pip's humble beginnings, has nothing to recommend him except his expectation of rank, and marries Estella, who is thus rewarded for the social superiority which had led her to hold the boy Pip in contempt. Estella in the end, when she and Pip re-meet in the grounds which are all that remain of Satis House, has, as Q.D. Leavis writes, 'gone through a process comparable with Pip's self-knowledge and humiliation so that they can truly come together at last'.[11] Both Pip and Estella have been taken out of the conditions of their birth; both have been the objects of the determinations of others; both have been battered in the process; and both have been brought to a clearer understanding of what is valuable in life. Both have found wealth and position to be of no comfort or protection against their potentially isolating effects. The novel's altered ending, from this point of view, seems to strike exactly the right note of muted optimism, though Peter Brook makes a case for preferring 'the original ending, with its flat tone and refusal of romantic expectation'.[12]

[11] Q.D. Leavis, 'How we must read *Great Expectations*', in F.R. and Q.D. Leavis, *Dickens the Novelist* (1970). Harmondsworth: Pelican Books, 1972, p. 426.

[12] Peter Brook, 'Repetition, Repression and Return: The Plotting of *Great Expectations*', in *Reading for the Plot: Design and Intention in Narrative* (1984), reprinted in Rosenberg (ed.) op cit, p. 687.

Myself, I support Mrs Leavis's contention about the original ending that it 'has the complete inconsequentialness of life, but is quite unsuitable for the conclusion of such a schematic novel'.[13] We might be wary of the word 'schematic' while accepting the tonal rightness of the tentative revised ending in which the inter-connected matters of class, wealth and morality find a quiet reso-lution. One of the major distinctions of this great novel is in the complexity of the perceptions it persistently exhibits in relation to how lives are shaped by such external circumstances as class and wealth and education as well as by inner qualities of sensitivity and instinct.

Dickens doesn't in *Great Expectations* fall into simplistic traps about salt-of-the-earth poor people and corrupt rich, or between pious lower orders and heartless upper classes. This is a work of Dickens's maturity: he was almost fifty when he wrote it and there were only two novels to follow (*Our Mutual Friend* and the unfinished *The Mystery of Edwin Drood*) before his death nearly nine years later in 1870. The kinds of sentimentality and unabashed melodrama that commanded a dominant place in some of the earlier works are here restrained and the discriminations have become much subtler. Yes, Joe is good but more intelligence and education might not have made him less so. Magwitch has been formed by an unjust society and had as a child struggled to live at all, but he is also genuinely alarming and Pip's repugnance when his benefactor returns and reveals himself is an entirely convincing response. Jaggers is a formidable figure in many respects, to criminals and others, but he also has a flinty insight into human wickedness and suffering that feels very like compassion. Miss Havisham is a half-mad grotesque but she is allowed, without

[13] Q.D. Leavis, op cit, p. 425.

softening the concept, moments of awareness of other needs, as when she allows Pip to intercede on Herbert's behalf. And so on.

In the quest that is Pip's moral trajectory as well as the more obvious one that will lead him eventually to the meeting in the ruined grounds of Satis House, he is not just an Everyman beset by emblematically drawn figures of good and evil. The fact that the chief influences on his development are not conceived in such binaristic terms makes his (unconscious) search for a decent way of living, a way of living that goes beyond self-gratification, more difficult for him and more rewarding for the reader.

Expectations – to have and have not

The title is ultimately ironic: for neither Pip nor Estella have the expectations of their youthful lives been fulfilled happily. Pip, on finding that Magwitch is his benefactor, can no longer accept the money that has precipitated him into the role of gentleman, though again the book is not suggesting that he would have been better off never to have left the forge. 'Dickens holds no brief for village life', Mrs Leavis remarks with succinct accuracy.[14] The sense in which he is finally better off is that he has made his own way, modestly, in the firm in which he'd persuaded Miss Havisham to make Herbert a partner, endowing Herbert thus with reasonable expectations to which he brings his own diligence and buoyancy. Magwitch's money has educated Pip in some social matters, has enabled him to widen his life's vistas, but has not equipped him to be more than a young man about town who runs up a list of creditors. Estella has been 'formed' by Miss Havisham for her own eccentric and vengeful purposes and, in the process of becoming admired by the male sex without herself being engaged by

[14] Ibid, p. 392.

anyone, she marries a socially acceptable boor who ill-treats her. Like Pip, she has been given expectations about the course of her life: the subdued ending of the novel is moving because of the recognition of how each of their lives has been wrenched out of its expected course, and because of the tentative strength this recognition has given them.

As far as Pip's situation is concerned, this gains a more complex resonance from the incidence of other young men who cross his path and the comparative and contrastive lights their progress or lack of it sheds on Pip. Orlick is the blacksmith's labourer to whom no one has ever proffered a helping hand. Julian Moynahan has written of Orlick in this regard: 'Up to a point, Orlick seems not only to dog Pip's footsteps, but also to present a parody of Pip's upward progress through the novel, as though he were in competitive pursuit of some obscene great expectation of his own ... (as he) moves his base of operations successively from the forge, to Satis House, and to London.'[15] Naturally surly, perhaps naturally vicious, no mollifying influence has gone to work on him. In the 1981 television version of the novel, the screenplay has Pip acknowledge 'Poor Orlick. He had a terrible life'. The line is not from Dickens but is acceptable as a marker of how far Pip has come in appreciating the lives and needs of others. So too is his interceding for Herbert with Miss Havisham, referred to above. Herbert will probably never enjoy huge success in the business world, but his honesty and total lack of jealousy in relation to Pip's expectations offer the nearest thing to a workable model for Pip. The incorrigible Trabb's boy, whom the burgeoning gentleman Pip finds so offensive, is the provincial lad who has neither

[15] Julian Moynahan, 'The Hero's Guilt: The Case of *Great Expectations*' (1960), reprinted in Norman Page (ed), *Hard Times, Great Expectations and Our Mutual Friend. A Casebook*. London and Basingstoke, Macmillan, 1979, p. 104.

aspiration nor expectation and whose natural resilience enables him utterly to accept his allotted place without envy and without acrimony, as he reveals when he leads the rescue party to save Pip's life at the hands of Orlick. Another provincial young(ish) man is the clerk Wopsle, who aspires to eminence as a preacher, if only the church were 'thrown open', and who finds his way on to the stage of an obscure London theatre where the limitations of his gifts are comically but not cruelly rendered. Significantly he has changed his name (to Waldengraver) as though this might enable him to remake his life. Drummle, as mentioned, is 'the next heir but one to a baronetcy' and has nothing to recommend him *but* his expectations and, Pip learns, 'had become quite renowned as a compound of pride, avarice, brutality, and meanness' and died 'from an accident consequent upon his ill-treatment of a horse' (Ch. LIX). The young man whose class-based position in life had seemed most clearly laid out has ended calamitously. In this network of reverberant echoes, it is perhaps also worth referring to Wemmick, who has maintained moral health by dividing his life into two: he leaves absolutely behind him the taint of Little Britain, and his contact with crime as Jaggers' clerk, when he returns home to Walworth where he cares devotedly for his senile old father.

Dickens does not parade this cast of comparators just to underline their significance in relation to his protagonist, but in their connections with him, realised for the reader in action that endows them with their own specificities, they help to inform our sense of Pip's development.

How is the story told
The narrator-hero
The one matter to which virtually all the novel's commentators have drawn attention is that of the first-person narration through

which everything is put before the reader. Everything we know about the people and events, and the reflections on these, we know through the words of the mature Pip – or rather the way in which Dickens works *through* him, for the narration is wittier and more penetrating than we might expect from Pip the character, unless we accept that he has matured remarkably in the years between his departure from England and his return. As the character grows nearer to the age of the narrating Pip, we may assume that there is less of a gap between what each perceives, but for the first third of the book Pip is a child, an adolescent and a very young man, and our perception of him at these stages of his life is gained through the recollections of his mature self, making what he can of his earlier experiences. We have to learn to trust that 'voice' and to make allowances for what the limitations of the character may impose upon it – and for how the voice 'escapes' the limitations of character. As Robert Garis has rhetorically asked: 'Who has ever "believed" that the famous comic set-pieces – Trabb's boy or Mr Wopsle's *Hamlet* – were the work of a man named Philip Pirrip, called Pip?'[16] As suggested above, though, this is (by comparison with some of Dickens's other novels) unusual in its concentration on its central character: he not only acts and is acted upon, but also must comment on and assess those acts.

So, what sort of voice has Dickens given to Pip? His earlier first-person narrator-protagonist, David Copperfield, had something of the function of autobiographer, drawing as he did on some aspects of Dickens's own life. As Anny Sadrin has written, he was free in that earlier book to give his narrator a voice like that of the author, 'But a new autobiographer, with a different name and a different

[16] Robert Garis, *The Dickens Theatre*. Oxford: Clarendon Press, 1965, p.191.

personality, would be expected to have a style of his own.'[17] In the novel's early chapters, there is a remarkable sympathetic alignment with the child's ways of thinking and feeling, without there ever being the slightest doubt that we are being given these through the voice of a much older man. And not only much older but one perceptive enough to feel for, as well as render, those infant terrors and the child's mortifications and growing sense of guilt and shame, and to be able to hold them in the perspective of Pip's whole spectrum of growth to the mature manhood which produces the narrator. A first-person narrator will in general need to be endowed with sufficient mobility of imagination, with a sufficiently acute perceptiveness, if the reader is not to feel confined by the narrating voice. (A modern novel, Graham Swift's *Last Orders*, addresses this problem by switching the voices: all the first-person narrators are more or less limited in their view of the past and none is especially articulate, but the action of the novel is partly in the conflicts generated by these disparate, partial accounts.)

Humphrey House famously wrote of the novel: 'It is, of course, a snob's progress; and the novel's greatest achievement is to make it sympathetic'.[18] The phrase 'a snob's progress' may seem a gross over-simplification of what happens to Pip, but the second part of the sentence certainly holds true. Dickens manages the precarious balancing act between the older Pip showing proper understanding of and remorse for his past errors of judgment and unworthy feeling, on the one hand, and what would be a too-moralising, breast-beating approach, on the other. Just occasionally the narrating voice can seem to be manoeuvring our sympathies

[17] Anny Sadrin, *Great Expectations*. London: Unwin Hyman Ltd, 1988, p. 184.

[18] Humphrey House, 'G.B.S. on *Great Expectations, Dickensian*, Vol. 44, 1948, reprinted in E. Rosenberg (ed) op cit, p. 644.

too overtly towards the now 'reformed' character of Pip, as for instance in some of his later dealings with Magwitch (e.g., 'For now my repugnance to him had all melted away ... (and) I only saw in him a much better man than I had been to Joe', Ch. LIV). But not often. The shrewdest statement of the first-person narrator I have found is Robert Partlow's, and it is so straightforward and clear that one wonders why no one else has put it in this way: 'In *Great Expectations* the narrator is neither Pip nor Mr Pip, but Mr Pirrip, a moderately successful, middle-aged businessman, a *petit bourgeois* who has risen in life by his own exertions and a fine bit of luck. Unlike the Pip of all but the last two chapters, he is a mature man, sober, industrious, saddened, aware of his own limitations, and possessed of a certain calm wisdom.'[19] The maintaining of the variable gap between the protagonist Pip and the narrating Pip/Mr Pip/Mr Pirrip is surely one of the book's triumphs.

One further point that might be added about Pip is that, interesting and sensitive as Dickens has made him, he is a curiously passive hero. His development is to a large extent a matter of his responding to influences, to being worked on by those who seek to hinder or advance him, rather than of his being the agent of his experience. Apart from his successful soliciting of Miss Havisham's help for Herbert, the two main occasions on which he notably 'acts' end in failure. He tries to rescue Miss Havisham from fire and he tries most earnestly to effect Magwitch's escape, but neither enterprise succeeds. He is alarmingly at the mercy of Orlick at the old sluice-house on the marshes and, so far from his being the kind of hero who rescues helpless victims, he has himself to be rescued by Herbert, the gentle Startop, and his old tormentor, the irrepres-

---

[19] Robert B. Partlow Jnr, 'The Moving I: A Study of the Point of View in *Great Expectations*', in Page (ed), op cit, p. 119.

sible Trabb's boy. My point here is that our interest in Pip is essentially less in what he does than in what he makes of his experiences, which brings me back to what I've called in the preceding paragraph, 'one of the book's triumphs': that is, to retain our sympathy with the Pip who is telling us the story even more than with the Pip who is the protagonist of it.

Realism, yes but ...

As far as 'The detailed presentation of appearances, especially of familiar experiences and circumstances',[20] to quote one definition of literary realism, is concerned, *Great Expectations* clearly exhibits the phenomenon in considerable measure. Think of how the opening scene of the marshes or Pip's first impression of London is presented. The marshes with the 'dark flat wilderness beyond the churchyard, intersected with dykes and mounds and gates, with scattered cattle feeding on it' (Ch. I), or Smithfield 'all asmear with filth and fat and blood and foam' and 'the roadway covered with straw to deaden the noise of passing vehicles' (Ch. XX) by Newgate. These are made vibrantly present through the detail with which they are observed, but in these two cases one also senses something more than realism at work. The image of the marshes, sensuously evocative as it is, quickly gives way to the sense of something more than realism in 'the distant savage lair from which the wind was rushing was the sea': it has become something ominous to the 'small bundle of shivers growing afraid of it all and beginning to cry' (Ch. I). And in the London moment, Pip turns into a street where 'I saw the great black dome of Saint Paul's bulging at me'(Ch. XX). I have deliberately not chosen occasions, such as the first glimpse of Miss Havisham or of Magwitch's return when a

[20] Barnet *et al*, op cit, p. 120.

more obviously gothic impulse is at work, but have selected examples of the way in which the realist almost imperceptibly slides into something more figurative, more symbolic in its representation than mere realism might produce.

In the matter of characterisation, while the reader acquires visually vivid images of a wide range of characters, the descriptive mode very often seems to be implying something more. Consider the account of Mrs Joe's

> trenchant way of cutting our bread-and-butter ... First, with her left hand she jammed the loaf hard and fast against her bib – where it sometimes got a pin into it, and sometimes a needle which we afterwards got into our mouths. Then she took some butter (not too much) on a knife and spread it on the loaf, in an apothecary kind of way, as if she were making a plaister – using both sides of the knife with a slapping dexterity, and trimming and moulding the butter off round the crust. Then, she gave the knife a final smart wipe on the edge of the plaister, and then sawed a very thick round off the loaf: which she finally, before separating from the loaf, hewed into two halves, of which Joe got one, and I the other. (Ch. II).

On a realist level we 'see' clearly what is going on, but the language goes beyond the realist to tell us important things about Mrs Joe. Words such as 'trenchant' and 'slapping' and 'a final smart swipe' reinforce our sense of this bullying woman's approach to everything. Notice, too, the way the word 'plaister' slides from the figurative ('as if she were making a plaister') to seemingly literal ('on the edge of the plaister'). The comparison of the buttering of the bread to the preparation of a 'curative application of some substance spread upon muslin, etc' (OED definition) in the first instance has acquired a different order of reality in the second. The whole description suggests the unnecessary rigour Mrs Joe brings to all her dealings with Joe and Pip: the preparation of food takes on a punitive edge in the particular usage of language Dickens favours. A similar process is at work in the description of Wemmick as Pip first observes him: 'I found him to be a dry man, rather short in stature, with a square wooden face, whose expression seemed to have been imperfectly chipped out with a dull-edged chisel. There were some marks in it that might have been dimples, if the material had been softer and the instrument finer, but which, as it was, were only dints. The chisel had made three or four attempts at embellishment over his nose ...' (Ch. XXI). What begins as a comparison, a subdued simile, with 'seemed to have been' ends as if it had slid into the 'reality' of 'The chisel had made ...' Again and again, we find the diction of the novel's narrating voice moving fluidly between the observably real and those other registers in which the metaphoric or the symbolic take over, and the reverse process as shown above is equally likely. Perhaps the Pip whose career we trace is never quite seen to be possessed of such nimbleness and wit: perhaps even 'Mr Pirrup', older and wiser as he is, might seem too life-worn for such dextrous flights. If so, we can only suggest that it is a convention one for the most part readily accepts.

Another attempt at explaining 'realism' claims: 'A thoroughgoing realism involves not only a selection of subject matter but, more importantly, a special literary manner as well: the subject is represented, or "rendered", in such a way as to give the reader the illusion of actual experience.'[21] In *Great Expectations*, however much Dickens may surround Pip with variously grotesque figures, the realist aspect of the novel is never wholly lost sight of in the

---

[21] Abrams, p. 153.

narrating language – and in the figure of the narrator-protagonist. Pip's experiences are rooted in recognisable realities – of aspiration, of humiliation, of disappointment – even where these are pushed into the forefront of his, and our, awareness by characters whose stranger, more obsessive ways serve purposes more emblematic and catalytic than that of securing the effect of what Henry James has called 'felt life'.

Challenges to the film-maker

If *Great Expectations* seems to offer irresistible appeal to film-makers, it also involves some challenges in its adaptation to the medium that 'shows' rather than 'tells'. Challenges, that is, if the film-maker aims at what is boringly called a 'faithful' film version of the original, and there is, it must be said, no compelling reason why they should. The film-maker who will excite us with his or her take on a classic novel will not be concerned about disturbing our personal responses to and mental images of the original; he or she will not be likely to want to stick as closely as possible to the literary antecedent, as if to do so were some sort of guarantee of quality. Orson Welles once remarked that he saw no point in adapting literature to the screen unless the film-maker had 'something new' to say about it.[22] With an author such as Dickens, there is too much chance of film-makers' feeling in awe of the original and the record of excitingly filmed Dickens is slight, and the intentions of the film versions of *Great Expectations* to be considered in later chapters do not appear to be in any serious sense radical.

[22] I can no longer find the source of this remark which is why I have not quoted it in full. My recollection was that he made it in conversation with Peter Bogdanovich in the 1970s, and I would be grateful if anyone can give me again the exact reference. The point remains a valid one, however.

Narrating voice

Some of the difficulties in adapting *Great Expectations* have been signposted in the discussion above. To start with, there is the question of the novel's first-person narration. For a film-maker who wants to retain this concentration on Pip's perceptions of the events and relationships of his own life, ways to replace at least the insistent commentary by more cinematic means will need to be found. Usual film practice tends to impose limits on the persistence of voice-over, which may seem the obvious way to treat first-person narration.

A kind of hero

Second, as heroes go, Pip presents a couple of problems, problems that may be more easily dealt with on the page than on the screen. For one, Pip is, as noted, for much of the novel less of an agent than a victim of other people's purposes, especially those of Magwitch and, as he supposes, of Miss Havisham, though of other lesser characters as well. The occasions on which he takes decisive action – as when he tries to save Miss Havisham from burning, or Magwitch from capture – are surprising for their rarity and lack of success, though they may be said to add to our sense of Pip's moral growth. Further, in relation to such larger-than-life characters as these (and Joe and Mrs Joe, Jaggers, Orlick and others) he can sometimes seem a somewhat shadowy figure. This can be countered by suggesting that his shadowiness is partly due to his being more ordinarily recognisable than the grotesques who cross his path and that they, in this way, have the advantage of flamboyant eccentricity whereas Pip must do with being 'ordinary'. A film will not too readily support the idea of a hero who lacks the vividness of the cast that surrounds him, and the casting of this central role will be crucially important. He is also a hero whom we watch in the process of his being formed while those around him are firmly set in their distinctive ways. A third problem with Pip as a potential film hero is that for much of the time he is not very likable: his shame about his origins and attempts to move into a higher level of society are made less damaging in the novel because there is the constant commentary of the mature Pip acting self-critically. How can film keep this kind of double perception in mind – and cause the viewer to have it in mind – if, that is, it wants to do so?

A muted ending

Another challenge relating to Pip and Estella is the book's subdued ending. In the last sentence of the revised ending, which Dickens incorporated on the suggestion of Bulwer Lytton,[23] he wrote: `... and in all the broad expanse of tranquil light they showed to me, I saw no shadow of another parting from her'. This very restrained and even ambiguous last clause (part of the 'happy ending' Dickens provided) is at some remove from the kind of closure expected of most popular commercial films. We shall see that most adaptations will favour something more positive than this.

A large cast

There is also the problem of what to do about so large a cast of characters, each of which in a 500-page novel can be given enough space to make a vivid impression. In a two hour film, it would obviously be necessary either to jettison a number of lesser characters (however entertaining or functional they may have been in the novel) or simply to reduce them to more or less

---

[23] See note re Dickens's original ending on last page of Thomas Nelson and Sons edition, p. 492.

meaningless walk-ons, though film can establish a good deal about a character in a few brief shots. Again, Lean was the film-maker who, arguably, dealt most effectively with this particular challenge, reducing some of the influences on Pip in order to highlight the major figures, and omitting the likes of Orlick and Trabb's boy whose importance in the novel is thematic rather than narratively crucial.

A filmable style?

More subtly, too, the novel offers a delusive suggestion that its intensely visual quality (e.g., in the account of Pip's first glimpse of Miss Havisham's house, both outside and in, or the description, referred to above, of Wemmick's features which looked 'carved in wood') will be a gift to the film-maker. In fact, looked at more closely these are often flights of metaphorical fancy, of a febrile verbal facility, rather than blueprints for screen transfer.

Nonetheless, however intransigent such problems may appear to be, it must be said that they have not conspired to cause film-makers to be wary of adapting *Great Expectations*, or indeed Dickens in general, to screens large and small, over a period of ninety years. Over-reverence to the original can virtually never be in the interests of film adaptation, and successful filming of Dickens cries out for a structurally, aesthetically and thematically radical approach. Much of the rest of this book will examine just how far film-makers have answered such a requirement.

Why was this novel filmed at these times?

It is interesting and possibly instructive to consider why *Great Expectations* should have appealed to film-makers at particular times. There is nothing conclusive about such speculations but they may throw some light on the kinds of adaptation that ensued. Did the 1917 version look forward to the end of war, to a time when a young man's chances might look more promising? Was the decision to make the 1934 film a response to the end of the Great Depression, again, if for different reasons, drawn to a story of a young man who has the prospect of good fortune to challenge him? I've always thought that David Lean's 1946 adaptation 'reads' like a metaphor for a better, less class-bound society in post-war England.

But it's not just a matter of how the films might respond to changing social/political climates that we should have in mind, but how the various adaptations emerge as products of their film-making contexts. Lean, for example, was working for the most pres-tigious production company in Britain at the time (perhaps at any time?), in a production climate which encouraged British cinema to pursue its literary and realist strengths. Joseph Hardy's 1975 version, a UK/US co-production, 'started out as a musical', according to its star, Michael York,[24] and was originally made for television, though it was later shown in cinemas. It was made at a low point in British cinema history when the mounting of an expensive period pro-duction might well have been difficult to achieve. Alfonso Cuarón's 1998 adaptation relocates the entire plot to modern-day Florida and New York, with stars who could attract international audiences. The mid-century challenge to Hollywood dominance, at least in British cinemas, was long since past, and it seems almost too neat that, eighty years after the first film of *Great Expectations*, made when the US was acquiring its dominance of world cinemas, the latest version was again a wholly American affair.

As far as the television series are concerned, four of these were made for the British Broadcasting Corporation (BBC) which, since

[24] 'Michael York' in Brian McFarlane (ed), *An Autobiography of British Cinema*. London: Methuen/BFI, 1977, p. 619.

the late 1950s, had established a reputation for the discreet serialisation of classic novels, those of Dickens and Jane Austen among the most popularly adapted authors. These mini-series have acquired over recent decades a probably unfair critical reputation for being merely safe, Sunday-night television fare, parading casts stuffed with notable character actors before (apparently) lavish production design. Whether it was for such reasons, or for the comfort associated with well-known titles (however *uncomfortable* such works might in fact be when closely examined) and the cachet associated with 'classic' literature, these serialisations were undeniably popular. In some ways, in their six- or twelve-episode formats, they offered an experience closer to the reading of long novels which inevitably have to be put aside at intervals for readers to get on with the rest of daily life, coming back to them again later as the television serial required one to do – and, of course, as Dickens required of the original readers of his serialised novels.

In the next section, I shall consider briefly some of the other sorts of afterlife that *Great Expectations* has inspired. Few novels can have given rise to so many 'hypertexts', in Gérard Genette's term: 'By hypertextuality, I mean any relationship uniting a text B (which I shall call the *hypertext*) to an earlier text A (I shall, of course, call it the hypotext), upon which it is grafted in a manner that is not that of commentary.'[25] As we shall see, some of the hypertexts to be discussed involve what Genette would characterise as 'transformation', which 'evokes more or less perceptibly without necessarily speaking of (the anterior text) or citing it'; others he would designate as 'imitation', a 'more complex process', which requires 'at

[25] Gérard Genette, *Palimpsests: Literature in the Second Degree* (trans. Chana Newman & Claude Doubinsky). Lincoln & London: University of Nebraska Press, 1982, p. 5.

least a partial mastery of (the anterior text), a mastery of that specific quality which one has chosen to imitate.'[26] Notions such as this, without dominating the discussion that follows, are useful for discriminating between different kinds of adaptation and in the case of *Great Expectations*, of adaptations in virtually every narrative medium, in very diverse circumstances and, possibly, with very different audiences in mind.

[26] Ibid, pp. 5, 6.

PART TWO:

From text
to screen

A note on the films

Unfortunately the silent film versions of *Great Expectations* have not been available for this study. My only recollections of 'silent Dickens' are of twenty years ago seeing Thomas Bentley's adaptation of *David Copperfield* (1913) and Maurice Elvey's of *Bleak House* (1921). Writing about these at the time, I noted that the former was little more than a hurtle through events, a series of tableaux filmed from a fixed camera and devoid of character elaboration and motivation. Elvey's film, however, was somewhat more sophisticated in its treatment, focusing on the story of Lady Dedlock and shearing away much of the rest.[1] Both films clearly missed the brilliance of Dickens's dialogue, without the cinema-specific resources of *mise-en-scène* and editing doing much to compensate, and both seemed to assume a certain knowledge of the original novels in their film audiences.

The sound films derived from *Great Expectations* are a mixed bag and they emanate from very different production circum-stances and social climates. This study is less concerned with evaluative judgments, though these inevitably emerge, than with offering some (comparative) sense of how film-makers over a period of sixty-four years (1934 to 1998) have responded to the novel and to the sorts of challenges it presents to a film-maker.

When one writes of 'challenges offer(ed) to a film-maker', such a phrase tends to suggest that the latter will be interested in some kind of cinematic rendering that aims at reproducing Dickensian effects in another semiotic system. The 'challenge' may not necessarily work towards that end; it is always possible for a film-maker to be excited by, inspired by, a particular aspect of a novel,

 [1] I have written briefly about these two films in 'A Literary Cinema? British Films and British Novels', in Charles Barr (ed), *All Our Yesterdays: 90 Years of British Cinema*. London: BFI Publishing, 1986, pp. 122–25.

and to use this aspect as his starting-point. Alfonso Cuarón's 1998 version is the one which most obviously 'takes off' from Dickens to pursue its interest in *Great Expectations*'s core plot in a very different setting and time. The 1934 version belongs to a period of profitable, conventional studio film-making; the 1975 had a rather curious genesis, it was intended for television and ended by being widely shown in cinemas. The 1946 film acquired almost instant classic status, all but deterring subsequent critical cavillings.

Taken together, these four films offer interestingly diverse approaches to the anterior text. No one 'approach' is *bound* to be more effective in film-making terms than another. Nevertheless, I think it is safe to say that, if the film-maker has no particular discernible purchase on the material, he will be unlikely to make a film either stimulating in its own right or as a transposition of an admired novel.

adaptations and extrapolations across the media

··

Given the multi-medial fascination with *Great Expectations*, it seems worth devoting a brief space to some of those 'adaptations' which do not conform to the usual idea suggested by the term but which have drawn their inspiration from this peculiarly rich and resonant novel. It seems likely that what follows does not exhaust the works that, in one guise or other, might claim the novel as a hypotext, but they will give some idea of how widely influential it has been.

On stage

In 1988 at the Glasgow Mayfest, there was a stage version described by theatrical author Jonathan Croall as 'brilliant'.[2] Staged by the Tag Theatre Company in association with the Gregory Nash group, it was directed by Ian Brown, with Nash as movement director and John Clifford as adaptor. A programme note by Brown and Nash describes the project as 'a rare collaboration between actors, dancers, musicians, composer, designer, writer, choreographer and director ... (during which) the piece has been able to

 [2] Letter to author, November 2005.

build slowly, the group experimenting with text, movement and voice ... (so as) to bring Dickens's world to the stage in a fresh and exciting way'.[3]

The Melbourne Theatre Company produced an utterly compelling four-hour re-telling of *Great Expectations* in 2002, in an adaptation by company director Simon Phillips and with a distinguished Australian cast and a minimalist but versatile set. One reviewer noted that 'Phillips has rightly exploited both the theatrical aspects of Dickens's writing and the special quality of the theatre itself to produce a satisfyingly rich and dense performance.'[4] This version of the novel included, ingeniously, the two recorded endings to the novel, settling finally with the happier one. It notably highlighted the theme of class-based inequities, insisting on the goodness of the poor and the cold egotism of those more advantageously placed in society. Phillips is on record as saying: 'It's ... the ultimate class story, about the potential for improvement and the potential for betrayal in the course of climbing up the social ladder.'[5] Another reviewer, less enthusiastic about the production over-all, nevertheless hinted at the enduring popularity of the original by reference to its generic hybridity: '*Great Expectations* is a thriller, a love story, a fable and a satire of Victorian Britain's class system.'[6]

In December 2005, the Royal Shakespeare Company's adaptation of *Great Expectations* (by the Cheek By Jowl founders, the

---

[3] Programme for Tag Theatre Company's adaptation of *Great Expectations*, Glasgow 1988.

[4] Helen Thomson, 'Cast rises to Dickens challenge', *The Age*, Melbourne, 26 September 2002.

[5] Simon Phillips interviewed in 'Expecting great things', *Preview*, September–October 2002, p. 15.

[6] Colin Rose, 'Dickensian pantomime', *Sun-Herald*, Sydney, 27 October 2002.

director Declan Donnellan and designer Nick Ormerod) opened at Stratford, with Siân Phillips as Miss Havisham in an otherwise not widely known cast. One critic described it as 'a wonderfully involving and eloquent adaptation', praising the way 'The cast double as a permanent chorus who, delivering lines in turn, take collective responsibility for the first-person narration, which sounds paradoxical but plays with great ease and naturalness.'[7] This last point is worth noting as the first-person is so crucial an element in the novel's tone and in anchoring its moral perceptions; and it is interesting to compare the theatre's directness in this matter with the more elaborate ways in which, say, David Lean goes about ensuring Pip's centrality to his film. Like Phillips in the Australian stage version, the RSC production also sees the story primarily in terms of class: 'Great Expectations is a story in which false ideas of what it is to be a gentleman are painfully stripped away.'[8] In both literary modes and in the human values Dickens's novel explores, espouses and dismisses, Great Expectations continues to speak tellingly to audiences of various kinds.

On the page

There is almost a sub-genre of literary fictions derived from classic novels or plays. Perhaps the most distinguished is Tom Stoppard's Rosencrantz and Guildenstern Are Dead (1966), which looks at the action of Hamlet through the eyes of the commonplace, finally out-manoeuvred courtiers of the title. There is real poignancy in Jean Rhys's Wide Sargasso Sea (1966), a post-colonial re-imagining of Charlotte Brontë's Jane Eyre from the viewpoint of the 'madwoman in the attic', the first Mrs Rochester. Haire-Sargeant's

[7] Paul Taylor, 'Expectations fulfilled this time', The Independent, 8 December 2005.
[8] Ibid.

Heathcliff: The Return to Wuthering Heights (1993) seeks to evoke his 'missing years' and does so in a narrative that belongs to pulp-fiction melodrama, a far cry from the gothic power of its progenitor. And last for the moment and certainly least, there is Emma Tennant's *Pemberley* (1993), a foolish and vulgar sequel to *Pride and Prejudice*.[9]

One might write in similarly derogatory terms of Michael Noonan's novel *Magwitch* (1982), which is a kind of sequel to *Great Expectations*, and which is narrated by Pip several years after his original narration had brought him to the point of return to his village and to Satis House after a decade in the east with Herbert's firm. In fact, the return to Satis House is now seen to have taken place after his visit to New South Wales. Noonan's Pip is still working for Clarriker's in Cairo but he has 'nursed a secret desire to make a journey of an altogether different kind, in another direction of the compass.'[10] 'Different', that is, from those painful journeys to England where he might meet 'Estella in the company of her husband.' He writes of 'my previous narrative', as if to establish himself as the chronicler of his own fortunes and this is probably a mistake on Noonan's part, as this Pip adopts an often laboured style of old-fashioned discourse in which 'both driver and postilion are apparelled in smart livery', a young woman speaks 'with a scornful toss of her dark tresses' and 'I deemed highly judicious that ...'[11] The effect is to draw attention to the glaring inferiority of this silly melodrama of hunting for Magwitch's hidden fortune in colonial New South Wales. The Pip

[9] Tom Stoppard, *Rosencrantz and Guildenstern Are Dead*, London: Faber and Faber, 1966; Jean Rhys, *Wide Sargasso Sea*, London: Deutsch, 1966; Lin Haire-Sargeant, *Heathcliff: The Return to Wuthering Heights*, London: Century, 1992; Emma Tennant, *Pemberley*, London: Hodder and Stoughton, 1993.

[10] Michael Noonan, *Magwitch*. London *et al*: Hodder and Stoughton, 1982, p. 7.

[11] Ibid., p. 11, p. 35; p. 96; p. 142.

who narrates this novel is a colourless romantic hero with none of the perception or wit of Dickens's narrating Pip.

In terms of plot, the novel has Pip show kindness in the Indian Ocean to a convict trying to escape on to the ship bearing Pip to Sydney, and this is one of the parallels the author uses to remind the reader of the book's antecedent. Another is to bring Pip into contact with the daughter of Magwitch and an Aboriginal woman, Charlotte, of the 'dark tresses.' Another is to position the flighty Charlotte as the foster-daughter of a rich vulgarian, Mrs Brewster, who proves to be the daughter of Miss Havisham. Also, Jaggers, having been transported for murdering his housekeeper Molly, is now installed as gate-keeper to the Rushmore estate, which has mysterious connections to Magwitch, and Jaggers, in an echo of his warning to Pip about revealing Estella's parentage, offers a similar caution about Charlotte's. *Magwitch* is full of unlikely secrets and unconvincing revelations, crowded with characters who make scant impression, and hurtles from one melodramatic incident to the next. However, it lacks the verve of real melodrama and the cohering power that Pip's sense of Magwitch's 'crazed romantic dream', to use Pip's phrase, might have given it in other hands, and the insight into the likely brutalities of Magwitch's colonial life, graphically enough suggested, are then fatally sentimentalised.

What matters about *Magwitch* is less its intrinsic merits than the further evidence it offers for the continuing fascination which Dickens's original narrative exerts. This fascination no doubt also accounts for Peter Carey's *Jack Maggs*, but this is a work of serious literary merit. The eponymous Maggs is Carey's version of Magwitch, a 'bolter' from New South Wales who has, like Dickens's character, returned perilously to London to see the gentleman he has 'made'. To re-establish contact with Pip, here called Phipps, he takes a position as footman in the London house next to Phipps's and makes rooftop sorties into the adjacent house, Phipps having vacated it in fear when he heard of his benefactor's return. Maggs, a man of violent monomaniacal temperament, terrorises the author Tobias Oates, a mesmerist who learns his secret and plans to write about it. If Carey is making his tale out of Dickens, Tobias makes *his* out of Carey, and at one point Maggs says, with ironic effect, 'You're just a character to me too, Toby'.[12]

There is a strong sense in this elliptic, idiosyncratic narrative of a post-modern take on a story of poverty, hardships, expectations, risings in society and the utter collapse of hopes. There is no place for sentimentality in Carey's tough-minded re-telling of the small boy who helps a convict out of terror and is, in return, made into a gentleman of epicene pusillanimity. Maggs has made his fortune in much more brutal ways (and is prepared to continue in them back in London) than Dickens suggests and, in Phipps, Pip's tendency towards extravagant indolence leads him to an ugly etiolation of the spirit. Carey is prepared to deconstruct the anterior text in the interests of revealing some of the realities that, in the words of one reviewer, 'were suppressed or unspoken in Dickens: homosexuality, illicit sexual passion, flogging of prisoners, the rape of child-prosti- tutes, and the abortion trade are unsentimentally exposed in this writing, as are Dickens's colonial assumptions.'[13]

Carey's book ends daringly with Maggs resettled in New South Wales, prospering in a country town where 'He was twice president of the shire and was still the president of the Cricket Club when Dick (son) hit the cover off a new ball in the match against Taree'.[14] It is as though Carey, in allowing Maggs a benign old age in New South

---

[12] Peter Carey, *Jack Maggs*. London: Faber and Faber, 1997, p. 280.

[13] Hermione Lee, 'Great extrapolations', *The Observer*, 28 September 1997.

[14] Carey, p. 327.

Wales, is offering both a Marxist and post-colonial revision of Dickens's scenario in which Magwitch is softened and transformed before he dies. For Carey, the old country is rife with class-based distinctions which all but predestine the likes of Maggs to poverty and crime, while the now recognises a different set of evaluative signifiers. In its way this could be seen as simply re-enshrining the Australian masculinist ethos which has valorised male hardihood in daunting circumstances and the notion that a man can make his way by dint of hard, uncomplaining work. If Dickens seemed to have little sense of the brutalities inherent in this anitpodean setting or of the role of women in it, Carey's revisionist account makes us re-think the story of expectations gratified and subverted. Hermione Lee is right to call *Jack Maggs* 'an imaginative and daring act of appropriation'.[15]

The most recent novel to draw on what the author must assume to be some kind of collective awareness of Dickens and of *Great Expectations* in particular is Lloyd Jones's *Mister Pip*, which was shortlisted for the Man Booker prize 2007.[16] Jones is a New Zealander but the book is published by an Australian company: it is almost as though Australia *needs* to maintain its connection with this novel. However, this quite enchanting piece of work is by no means a re-telling of its famous antecedent from another point of view; it works more imaginatively than that. It is set on the island of Bougainville from which all but one white, an unprepossessing, awkward man called Watts, have departed and the island has been terrorised by military incursions from Port Moresby and by its own rebel guerrillas. The central character and narrator is a girl called Matilda (roughly ten, at the novel's start), named surely in reference to the way her

15 Lee, op cit.

16 Lloyd Jones, *Mister Pip*. Melbourne: The Text Publishing Company, 2006.

father has 'gone Australian' and gone to work in Queensland when the island's mine has closed down. Watts, with no qualifications for the job, sets up a school on the island and thereby helps to fill the lives of the children left there. He does rather more than this implies: his only teaching aid appears to be a copy of *Great Expectations* which he reads to them at the rate of a chapter a day. When the book disappears (hidden by Matilda's mother Dolores, who fears its unsettling influence), Watts encourages the children to piece the narrative together from their recollections, and another sort of adventure in narrative begins.

The links between Matilda and Pip are spelt out in her own words:

> At some point I felt myself enter the story. I hadn't been assigned a part – nothing like that, I wasn't identifiable on the page, but I was there, I was definitely there. I knew that orphaned white kid and that small fragile place he squeezed into between his awful sister and loveable Joe Gargery because the same space came to exist between Mr Watts and my mum. And I knew I would have to choose between the two.[17]

She will eventually, like Pip, leave the familiar island of her childhood, journey first to Australia, and then, like Pip again, will venture upon London and find grounds for disillusionment. But Watts, too, is also taken for Pip by the invading 'redskins': in a sense, he has made a comparable journey, having come from white England via New Zealand, to the island where he cares for a crazed black wife. He is also Miss Havisham and Jaggers, opening up new worlds for Matilda; at one point Matilda fears he has 'gotten his characters

[17] Ibid., p. 40.

mixed up, that somehow he had slipped out of Pip and into Joe Gargery's skin';[18] and he pays with his life for having become identified with the eponymous Mister Pip. This isn't the place for a full-scale analysis of the many felicities of Jones's delicate but rigorous account of a life expanding under the influence of another, fictional life. Matilda may, in London, have 'fallen out of love with his (Mr Dickens's) characters',[19] but he has left her with a more important legacy:

> ... my Mr Dickens had taught every one of us kids that our voice was special, and we should remember this whenever we used it, and remember that whatever else happened to us in our lives our voice could never be taken away from us.[20]

It is perhaps not too much of a stretch to claim that the original Pip's growth is at least in part a matter of having found *his* own voice and that the reader can assess how far Pip has grown by listening to it carefully.

Last and least of these novelistic extrapolations is Sue Roe's *Estella: Her Expectations*. This affectedly 'poetic' work has only tangential connections with Dickens as it explores the inner life of an Estella who is perhaps the most solipsistic heroine in English – possibly *all* – literature. This Estella answers an advertisement for a room in the dusty house that belongs to a woman, a dancer who 'has seen Paris ... where Diaghilev redesigned the lines and textures of the body, and made it dynamic'.[21] She becomes fascinated with

[18] ibid., p. 156.
[19] ibid., p. 218.
[20] ibid., p. 220.
[21] Sue Roe, *Estella: Her Expectations*. Brighton, Sussex: Harvester, 1982, p. 7.

this Havisham figure, decks herself, while the dancer is out, in the faded remnants of her life, including the wedding gown. As this is ostensibly a feminist text, the dancer has not been jilted but has called off the wedding the day before it was due to take place. Estella spends a great deal of time, in prose of tiresome fragment-ariness, searching for herself in mirrors, in imagining a gypsy lover, in reading a book about images of women.[22] Pip in this story is a small boy learning to dance, and by the end of the book he is still a child, playing on the beach. In the book's penultimate 'Part', he watches as the mists filter the light and Estella leaves for Paris: 'She is sure to come back, one warm, bright day when he will have changed, grown up, and she will have stayed the same.'[23] There are other fleeting references to *Great Expectations* ('What larks! They laugh.'[24]), but this perception of Pip always being younger than Estella, then growing up to be her equal, may be Roe's most tantalising connection to Dickens. By contrast with the latter, *Estella: Her Expectations* tends to read as if Gertrude Stein was having a go at writing a romantic novel – and failing. It is only worth noting here as yet another example of the extraordinarily prolific heritage of Dickens's novel.

One further 'adaptation' of *Great Expectations* to the page is in Rosalind Ashe's *Literary Houses*.[25] The second chapter of this handsomely illustrated text is devoted to a paraphrasing of Miss Havisham's story and to details about the nature and structure of Satis House. There are 'architects' plans' of the ground and first

[22] Ibid., p. 41.

[23] Ibid., p.149.

[24] Ibid., p. 39.

[25] Rosalind Ashe, *Literary Houses*. Limpsfield: Dragon's World Ltd, 1982, pp. 29–37. The illustrations are copyrighted to Dragon's World, not to individual artists.

floors, black-and-white sketches of the exterior of the house and of the adjoining ruins of the malthouse, and rather beautiful coloured imaginings of the cobwebby desuetude within.

A brief note is needed for Rick Geary's 'Classics Illustrated' adaptation in 1990,[26] a version that might be valuable for interesting young readers in Dickens. In what could be described as graphic-novel format, this is written almost exclusively in Dickens's language, and the illustrations, perhaps looking more American than English, are characterful and sustained. One small point that caught my attention was the similarity between the way Mrs Joe has been imagined and that in which Miss Havisham is depicted. Is the author intending to suggest two different but malign female influences at work on the young Pip? The young Pip and Estella are more or less devoid of character, but those surrounding them are imbued with a nice sense of gothic exaggeration which seems true to the spirit of the great original. It begins to seem that *Great Expectations* has cast a wide net of fascination, the tree that Dickens planted having ramified into a much wider world of the arts.

On radio

There have been several radio adaptations of *Great Expectations*, including at least half a dozen BBC versions since it was first adapted by Mabel Constanduros and Howard Agg, produced by Raymond Raikes, as a twelve-part serial on Home Service Sundays (evenings), beginning 19 September 1948. There were also a further twelve-part serial in *Calling West Africa* (Colonial Service) beginning on 2 October 1951; a seven-part serial on *Children's Hour*, adapted

---

[26] Rick Geary, *Charles Dickens Great Expectations*, Classics Illustrated. New York: Berkeley Publishing Group, 1990.

by H. Oldfield Box, from 12 January 1958; a twelve-part serial also adapted by Box and produced by Robin Midgley on the Home Service (scheduled for tea-time audiences) from 16 April 1961; and an eight-part Sunday Serial (evenings), adapted by Charles Lefeaux, starting 21 September 1975. The timing of these seriali-sations (and how apt Dickens is for such treatment) suggests that those programmes, scheduled at tea-time or early-to-mid evening, were probably occupying slots that would increasingly become the province of television series/serials. However, more recently (May 1998) there was a (three-part, each 30 minutes) BBC radio serialisation on consecutive Monday nights at 8pm, repeated at 11am early in the following year. It would seem that a change in listening priorities had occurred, possibly in response to the omni-potence of television. Apart from such serialisations, there was a ten-part serial reading in Radio 4's *Story Time*, the abridgement written by Howard Jones and produced by Trevor Hill.[27]

A television extrapolation

Not strictly an adaptation of the kind that will be considered in the next chapter, the Australian mini-series, *Great Expectations: The Untold Story* (1986), albeit more cryptically, has Magwitch restored like Carey's Maggs to Australia, with the purpose, according to script editor Tom Burstall, of reflecting what the film-makers saw as 'the convict basis of some of Australia's egalitarian values'.[28] As that literary sub-genre referred to above suggests,

[27] Most of the data in this paragraph comes from Trish Hayes, Archives Researcher, Written Archives Centre, BBC Information & Archives, in a letter to the author, December 2005.

[28] Interview with the author, Melbourne, December 2005, the source of other unattributed quotations in this section.

there are always aspects of novels which, for whatever reason, the author has not developed. So, one reads *Jane Eyre* and wonders how the first Mrs Rochester came to be there in the attic. What, one ponders, and as Jean Rhys obviously once pondered, is *her story*? In *Great Expectations*, one of the 'untold stories' is Magwitch's. We are given his account of it in a few pages at the end of the novel's second 'stage', but it is all a matter of telling rather than drama- tising. It is Pip's story that is *enacted* before us there. Of Tim Burstall's mini-series, his son Tom said, 'We wanted to make Magwitch the central character. Our film was being done from his perspective, and this was to be an Australian perspective.' For a while in the early 1980s there were attempts to get the film made in the US and later in England, but the Burstalls wanted it to be an essentially Australian enterprise and resisted such offers as they received. In the end, there was some UK financing from Hemdale Film Corporation, the company formed by David Hemmings and John Daly, but creatively the series was entirely an Australian production. And as far as finance goes, it was mainly the work of producer Tony Ginnane whose 'sophisticated approach to film financing' was respected.

If Carey in the end seems to dispense with the idea of 'What is a gentleman?' revealing cruelty and folly across the class range in a very twentieth-century way, Tim Burstall wanted this question to be at the heart of his *Untold Story*. The Burstalls were fascinated by Dickens's connections to Australia, and, though his knowledge of the country was limited to 'books and verbal description',[29] it assumes a metaphoric role in his novel as a place where a man might do well, though he'd been a ne'er-do-well in England. Further, two of his sons, Alfred and his favourite Edward, migrated to Australia. Alfred went first and eventually owned a sheep station

[29] Peter Ackroyd, *Dickens*. London: Sinclair-Stevenson Ltd, 1990, p. 1032.

and Edward, to his father's grief, followed several years later. In another minor connection, the novelist Justine Larbalestier claims that 'the grave of the reputed original for Miss Havisham', Eliza Emily Donnithorne, is to be found, now restored after being vandalised, in St Stephen's cemetery, Newtown, Sydney.[30] Whether true or not, this bit of trivia perhaps points again to the Australian fascination with *Great Expectations*. In fiction, Dickens seems to have been tempted by the wish to see what those despised in England might achieve in a new country. John O. Jordan has said: 'The shadow of Dickens falls heavily across the Australian literary and cultural production of the past two centuries'[31] and one wishes he'd had space to develop this thesis at greater length, but he is right in singling out *Great Expectations* as the key novel in this respect. *Untold Story* picks up Dickens's vague sense of how a new life might be forged away from centuries-ingrained patterns of social division and expectation.

The way the Burstall mini-series deals with Dickens is almost like a photographic negative in the relation it bears to the original novel. By this I mean that it uses the original material more or less minimally: approximately one hour of the six-episode mini-series dramatises episodes directly taken from the novel. The rest highlights what is 'off-page' (to use a term suggested by the common 'off-screen') in the novel: that is, essentially the events which concern Magwitch's antipodean career. When Burstall draws on Dickens, he generally adheres to it with a tenacity in matters not only of incident but also of dialogue that would satisfy the most fidelity-driven viewer. In a

[30] Gwenda Bond, 'The Original Miss Havisham', 11 November 2004, www.justinelarbalestier.com/Musings/Musings2004/cemetery.htm
[31] John O. Jordan, '*Great Expectations* on Australian television', in John Glavin (ed), *Dickens on Screen*. Cambridge: Cambridge University Press, 2003, p. 46.

1986 interview, he said that he 'sticks to Dickens exactly' in those episodes chronicled in the original, but that 'I can invent material about what happens out in Australia that fits in'.[32] However, he does not follow Dickens's lead in every matter relating to Magwitch in England, most notably in the playful ending, and there are also moments relating to Pip (say, at Miss Havisham's) which have nothing to do with Magwitch, at least as far as is known at that point.

It is, as Jordan says, 'at once an adaptation of Dickens's novel and an imaginative expansion of it'.[33] In fact, it might be true to say that it is *less* an 'adaptation' than 'an imaginative expansion'. It opens with credits over a series of dark Doré etchings of city life[34] and it ends in the brightly lit open countryside of Australia, with Jaggers and Wemmick laughing heartily as their carriage rattles along. The aesthetic differences between the two images are significant. *Untold Story*'s sympathies are essentially antipodean and the contrasting images – the one crowded and squalid, the other sunny and rural – and the way they are lit and their placement at the opposite ends of the mini-series underlines this. And this is allied to the series' representation of class matters. Its narrative starts at a race meeting in which Magwitch (John Stanton) is captured by police after passing a forged £1 note. In the subsequent trial scene, Jaggers (Noel Ferrier), now a barrister, undercuts Compeyson's gentlemanly surface, calling him a 'natural rogue' and makes a plea for Magwitch, 'the natural gentleman', based on his harrowing life story. The judge, however, is unmoved by Jaggers' criticism of the class system, persists in seeing Compeyson as misled, and lets

---

[32] Tim Burstall on *The 7.30 Report*, Australian Broadcasting Commission, September 1986.

[33] Ibid., p. 47.

[34] Tom Burstall in discussion with the author.

him off with seven years' transportation while Magwitch, who looks and talks like a low-life, is condemned to fourteen.

All this precedes Magwitch's graveyard meeting with Pip. In New South Wales, Magwitch, having endured the rigours of the chain-gang, is assigned to work for landowner Tankerton (Ron Moody), who so comes to value his services that he helps to make him rich. Magwitch's career prospers, his growing wealth earmarked to make Pip a 'gentleman'. The notion of what constitutes a gentleman is explored throughout, with Magwitch emerging as one by nature and Compeyson as a scoundrel with nothing but the outward accoutrements. This shifting connection between wealth and position on the one hand and true gentlemanliness on the other is of course one of Dickens's major preccupations; in *Untold Story*, the genuine article comes to be equated, perhaps chauvinistically, with Australia, which is represented as a crucible in which a man's real virtues, regardless of his birth-class, might have a chance to emerge.

The England/Australia dichotomy is reflected not only in such thematic articulations but in matters of composition and lighting. Australia inevitably *looks* like a land of opportunity, once it breaks free of the brutalities of convict labour and cruel punishment. As a stepping-stone towards the moral reclamation of Magwitch, he is offered the chance of pardon if he will act as hangman to other convicts but refuses it, saying 'I couldn't do it'. In his work on Tankerton's property, he acquits himself efficiently but without any sycophancy. There is a spaciousness about the vistas in the colony that contrasts with the cramped life of London and the gloom of Pip's marsh country. The early scenes there, with a terrified Pip (always depicted in a warm glow that gives the child a saintly look in contrast with the threat of Magwitch in these early encounters) are reprised at the end of the first episode in a montage of memories as Magwitch reflects on his answer to the question put to him: 'Has no one ever done you a kindness?'

Misplaced loyalty to a fellow-convict, even to one he hates, prevents him until too late from revealing Compeyson's past to Tankerton, whose daughter (Sigrid Thornton) he hopes to marry and whose life he ruins when he elopes with her. The film may be endorsing popular Australian values but it doesn't shirk the hard-ships of the colonial life or the dangers of the country, often hostile to human endeavour. However, its reworking of the conclusion leaves us clear about where its chief sympathies lie. If so formidable an Englishman as Jaggers settles eventually for its wide open spaces, he who has been the terror of Inner London's seedier denizens, and if Magwitch is restored there (the series maintains a nicely ambiguous approach to this), then it is possible to see his evolution from convict-on-the-run to rugged outback hero as offering a paradigm for the growth of the colony. Jordan may well be right when he claims that *Untold Story* 'is nothing less than an attempt to dramatise the founding of the nation'.[35] The Burstalls may not have conceived of their project in quite such grandiose terms, but in the arduous challenges of the new colony there is a real sense of possibilities which the old country can no longer reliably offer.

In this 'photographic negative' approach to Dickens's novel, Pip (Danny Simmonds as child, Todd Boyce as adult) has little more than an emblematic role. He grows from one of those sweetly-spoken Dickensian children (not for them the common or regional accents of those around them) into the extravagant young man-about-town on the proceeds of the 'expectations' he has had from Magwitch. *Untold Story*, in a few neatly sketched scenes,

[35] Jordan, p. 47.

traces his passion for Estella (Anne Lambert). Chilled into emotional irresponsiveness as a result of her training by Miss Havisham (Julia Forster), she puts Pip through the prescribed humiliations and jealousies. Burstall has known how much of Pip's story – the *told* story – he needs to include so that the reunion with Magwitch many years later, on a wild London night, will have its climactic importance, for both men – for the 'made gentleman' and the 'natural gentleman'. Jessop (Alfred Bell), Magwitch's Australian lawyer, is still near enough to his English background to warn Magwitch when the latter plans to reveal himself to Pip: 'You've taken him out of his class. He's inherited a great deal of property. What do you think he'll feel when he finds out the source?' And Pip's pompous, fearful speech about 'amending your way of life' when he does so, confirms Jessop's apprehensions.

Pip still tries to rescue Magwitch, as in the novel, but the emphasis is now less on Pip's moral reclamation than on Magwitch's subsequent dealings with Compeyson whose machinations he counters with: 'I won't be threatened. I won't be blackmailed. I'm not about to have my spirit broken by scum like you.' Spoken, if not exactly like a gentleman, at least like a man with a firm sense of his own selfhood, a selfhood Burstall's screenplay and direction would have us accept as the product of his years in the new colony as yet unshackled by class. In John Stanton's quietly charismatic rendering of Magwitch, Burstall's apparent intentions are persuasively realised. The novel's preoccupation with true gentlemanliness is given an extra dimension when filtered through a new, post-colonial viewpoint: that, rather than slavish reverence to an original, however distinguished, is the kind of difference that justifies adaptation of a well-loved classic.

The animated version

On the face of it, *Great Expectations* seems an unlikely candidate for a 70-minute animated adaptation, but Burbank Films, an Australian company which frequently ventured into the field of classic fiction, thought otherwise. It also made, for instance, *Oliver Twist, The Old Curiosity Shop, Nicholas Nickleby, David Copperfield, A Christmas Carol* and *The Pickwick Papers* all in 1984–85.[36] On the basis of the company's version of *Great Expectations*, it is clear that their product is intended for children, and children could have a much worse introduction to Dickens.[37] Of course the plot is wildly simplified; of course the characters are essentially one-dimensional; and of course the novel's thematic richness is diluted almost to the point of non-existence: nevertheless, the film has a certain charm and narrative verve that would recommend it to young audiences.

The plot outline is, for the most part, preserved, though inevitably a good many major events and encounters from the original are missing. The film whizzes through such cardinal narrative functions as Pip's churchyard meeting with Magwitch, the hunting down of the convicts by the soldiers, Pip's being taken to Satis House where he meets Miss Havisham, Estella and, later, Herbert, his transformation into a 'gentleman', the return of Magwitch, the attempt to send him to safety (not, oddly, to be accompanied by Pip), and Pip's return after this aborted enterprise to his village where he re-meets Estella. All this is present in the broadest outline, events such as Mrs Joe's death being recorded with no explanation and the

[36] Information provided by David Field, Managing Director of the current Burbank Animation Studios Pty Ltd, Sydney, in discussion with the author, January 2006.

[37] On its website, www.burbankanimation.com.au, the company claims to be: 'A company devoted to the production of Entertaining Animated Films for the children of the world and the young at heart.'

business of Pip's receiving his expectations being no sooner announced than he is seen on the mail coach for London. There are flashbacks explaining how Miss Havisham was jilted, and how Magwitch was corrupted by Compeyson and caught passing forged banknotes, such episodes presumably in the interests of clarifying events for very young viewers.

Events is what they are, no more nor less. They are simply, as one would expect, links in a clear narrative chain, not stages in Pip's growth. He changes physically but there is no sense of his losing sight of his moral bearings (except in a brief moment of silent reproach from Biddy) or of his need for reclamation as he reacts to Magwitch's return. Pip and Estella (and Biddy) are drawn as vacuous Disney-ish figures devoid of character, so that it is surprising that after their final meeting in the ruins of Satis House they part. 'You've become a gentleman', says Estella. 'And I'm going back to London', he replies, 'to become something else – myself'. Perhaps this is the film's belated recognition of the dramatic course of Dickens's fiction.

The drawing of the characters is generally uninspired, though the surrounding figures have more life than the protagonists. An unusually plump Miss Havisham (spelt Haversham) suggests the sort of the haughty upper-class types played by actresses such as Irene Browne; Jaggers has a jowly conviviality as he talks of boys as being generally 'a bad set of fellows'; and Magwitch is alarming enough at first, acquiring avuncular benignity later. And so on. One nice innovative touch is that Trabb's boy has now become Trabb's 'girl', a freckled 'common' village girl who mocks Pip.

The animation is not remarkable, especially in the context of twenty-first-century developments in the field, but there is some real charm in its evocation of place. In the church graveyard of the opening sequences, there is some sense of 'borrowing' from Lean's version, with boughs creaking in the wind which is reinforced on the soundtrack, and in the way Pip collides with Magwitch as he makes to run home from the churchyard. The colour palette of the early marsh scenes is limited to sandy browns and when the church appears it takes on a touch of gentle gothic. Against the empty Disney-esque faces of the young leads, the drawing of the village or of an idealised London has some of the grave charm of Edward Ardizzone's illustrations for children's books. And some of the scenes by the river, particularly one in which Pip and Herbert cross the river to see a transpontine melodrama called, aptly enough, 'Fortune's Ladder', have real merit of what is probably a rather old-fashioned kind.

The adaptation is by the Australian playwright, Alex Buzo, with Jean Tych and Warwick as chief animators, supplemented by a large team, and the voices of the cast include the Australian actors Bill Kerr, Moya O'Sullivan and Philip Hinton (who also had a small role in Tim Burstall's *Great Expectations: The Untold Story*), and the composer, Richard Bowden, is also Australian. The film, made in 1983, released a year later, then appears to be the work of Burbank's Australian studios, in spite of the BFI's Film Index International's attributing it to the US. As a film it is only worth noting in the context of this book for what further evidence it suggests of the enduring appeal of Dickens's original story and for the character it brings to places if not to faces, but, again, it may bring young viewers to an interest in Dickens.

great expectations
on television

••

It might almost be said that the mini-series was invented for the visual realisation of Dickens. As an author who consciously – and with great commercial success – wrote for serial publication, the aim being, whatever other loftier intentions, to keep readers coming back for more, he would surely have welcomed with delighted enthusiasm the prospect of a medium designed to beguile viewers with the promise of weekly instalments in their own homes. In structural terms, the serial treatment requires an element of coherence and autonomy in each episode while bearing in mind its place in the larger scheme of the whole novel. Further, each instalment needs its own sense of climax, the product perhaps of a revelation or a turning point in a relationship or a crucial plot move, as well as leaving the reader with a narrative question to be answered in the next. In some ways, then, the expansiveness of a long, rich novel such as *Great Expectations*, originally published in thirty-six weekly instalments,[1] would seem, in theory at least, to be more easily adaptable to the demands of the television 'serial' or 'mini-series', as it is usually called, than to those of the single movie, of roughly two hours running time.

 [1] In *All the Year Round*, from December 1860 to August 1861.

Great Expectations is one of Dickens's most sophisticated and complex works and it does not characteristically engage in the kind of cliff-hanger endings associated with popular serials. The chapter (XLIV) that ends with Pip's receiving Wemmick's note: 'DON'T GO HOME' is exceptional in its charged melodramatic flourish; the following chapter is more typical in ending with '... and I inferred from the number of tea-cups, as well as from his glances at the two little doors in the wall, that Miss Skiffins was expected' (Ch. XLV). The chapters, that is, tend to finish on a note of reflection, or quiet anticipation, rather than a pitch of excitement, though the actual instalments did not necessarily conclude where a chapter ends. The three main sections, the 'stages' of 'Pip's expectations', are similarly reflective, drawing on aspects of weather: 'the mists had all solemnly risen now ...' at the end of the first stage, as Pip sets out for London; '... the wind and rain intensified the thick black darkness', at the end of the second as Pip contemplates the return of Magwitch; and at the novel's end 'the evening mists were rising now': there is obvious care in the organisation of these stages and how they finish. Nevertheless, the rich texture of the *action* of the novel suggests its amenability to the mini-series format: though it is for Dickens unusually single-minded in its focus on its protagonist and resistance of subplots, it is very rich in characters who, vivid in themselves, are all important in narrative or thematic terms to Pip's growth. Even David Lean's famous film adaptation was forced to omit numbers of these and give short shrift to others. This is not to suggest that a television mini-series will automatically give greater insights into the story it adapts; merely that it offers more scope for rendering the almost profligate fruits of Dickens's imaginative genius.

The literary mini-series has been a staple of British television (and no doubt that of other countries) since the 1950s, and the first of the five mini-series versions of *Great Expectations* was in 1959, premiered by the BBC on 5 April, and starring Dinsdale Landon and Helen Lindsay as the adult Pip and Estella. There were four further: two more for the BBC, in 1967 with Gary Bond and Francesca Annis in the leads and in 1981 with Jerry Sundquist and Sarah-Anne Varley; a BBC-WGBH Boston co-production, in which the young leads are overshadowed by the *réclame* of Jean Simmons as Miss Havisham and Anthony Hopkins as Magwitch; and another UK/US co-production (involving Harlech TV and Disney) in 1999. Of these five, I have some recollections of the 1967 version whose opening so closely mirrored Lean's and the starrily cast 1989 one which had a special poignancy in the casting of Jean Simmons, the young Estella in Lean's film, as Miss Havisham. However, only two of the five have been available for this study: the 1981 and 1999 adapt-ations, and fortunately they exemplify very different approaches to the enterprise. The 1981 mini-series is a long (288 minutes), solidly traditional rendering of its great antecedent, while the 1999 retelling offers a shorter (180 minutes), more radical approach. Both in their respective, disparate ways have a good deal to offer.

Great Expectations (1981)
Director: Julian Amyes; screenplay: James Andrew Hall

As one who is normally of the view that the most valuable film adaptations of literary works are those that engage in bold re-imagining of the original, I must admit to taking a great deal of sheer pleasure in this leisurely, well-crafted version. It is conventional enough in terms of what one expects of BBC serialised versions of the classics: it is in every sense careful in relation to the precursor text; somehow, though, it manages to offer more than just a filming-by-numbers approach. Traditional in its adherence to both the overarching patterns and, very often, to the details of Dickens's story, it also exhibits traditional virtues of clear story-telling, intelligent production design and some excellent performances from a well-chosen cast. And, traditional as it is in most ways, it can still sometimes surprise one with the astuteness of its interpretations and by moments of real feeling.

Like most versions for screens large and small, it starts with the confrontation in the marshes between Pip and the convict Magwitch, and again like most versions it makes use of the voice-over of the mature Pip.[2] There is a nicely evocative opening shot of the older Pip, in silhouette, contemplating his childhood self coming into the graveyard, thus in a sense providing a parallel to the novel's device of the older Pip as narrator of his younger fortunes. This announces at once the centrality of Pip as both protagonist and chronicler. He reads in voice-over the epitaph on the tombstone about father and sons and in doing so foreshadows one of this version's emphases. The Magwitch in Amyes' mini-series is an appropriately threatening figure in Stratford Johns's performance and the dialogue here, as indeed throughout the whole of the first 'stage' of the production, follows Dickens very closely, to the point where you anticipate the next line. This kind of fidelity (that tiresome word again) characterises Amyes' rendering of all the main narrative moves of the novel's first third: the Christmas dinner (with the brilliantly absurd dialogue about 'swine' and youthful ingratitude preserved intact, brought to a halt – as always in the adaptations – by the soldier at the door), the struggle between the convicts in the mud and the exchange of looks between Pip and Magwitch; the visit to Satis House, with an authoritative, less 'mad' Miss Havisham and an Estella (played by the young Patsy Kensit) who, as usual

[2] The only exception I am aware of is the 1999 mini-series, discussed later.

seems much older than Pip; the arrival of Jaggers, glimpsed at Satis House, later at the forge with news of Pip's expectations, thus rounding off the first stage and, with the promise henceforth of (as the voice-over records) 'London and riches', ushering in the second.

If you compare this with the list of 'major cardinal functions', in Barthes's term, quoted earlier,[3] it will be seen that, apart from the appearance of the stranger at the inn who stirs his beer with Joe's file, nothing of narrative consequence has been omitted, and this holds good for the series as a whole. This is not a matter for praise or disapproval, merely a statement about the kind of adaptation with which we are here dealing. The allocation of running time between the three stages of the novel is much more evenly done than usual, the film versions in particular tending to privilege the opening stage leading up to Pip's departure for London, and to deal somewhat elliptically with the matters of Pip's London education and his subsequent redemption. Here they are given roughly equally time and weight. And scarcely a character from the novel's large cast fails to get his or her moment of screentime: for instance, Orlick, missing from the film adaptations, assumes the novel's importance here; the Pocket household is represented in its chaos and delusory aspirations; even Wemmick's intended, Miss Skiffins, is briefly present. All this has nothing to do with adaptation theory, but perhaps it is common enough to enjoy seeing how remembered events and characters have been perceived by others with access to another medium of representation.

So what, if anything, gives distinction to this long, often talkative (that sounds pejorative, but it is hard to object to Dickensian dialogue spoken with wit or feeling and understanding) recreation

[3] See pp. 9–11 for this list.

of the novel, a rendering in Grahame Smith's words of 'a narrative of consciousness across different media and across time'?[4] Amyes' production does not offer a daringly individual reading of the work as a whole, but there are several ways in which this version provides the stimulus of new perceptions of well-known events and characters and their interaction. There is, for example, a strong emphasis on the concept of what may shape the futures of young men in different circumstances. Pip, obviously, is the focus for this interest, but this adaptation significantly extends it to consider the fates of Orlick, Herbert, Wopsle, and even of Wemmick. The treatment of Orlick (Lionel Haft) is particularly striking. Here is a young man who never has any expectations and is embittered by what he sees of the limitations of his life. In the series from a very early scene in the forge, his resentment of what he sees as Pip's privileged position ('you sneaking little devil' he later abuses Pip) reflects oddly on Pip's own view of his inadequate, 'common' circumstances, and when Orlick finally confronts Pip in the old boathouse on the marshes there is a powerful sense of Orlick's displacement as result of Pip's intervention in his life. The scene would be still more unsettling if Jerry Sundquist's Pip had more dramatic stature, but even so Orlick's account of how he struck down Mrs Joe has a genuinely disquieting resonance. 'It was done through *you* ... It wasn't old Orlick as done it. It was *you*.' Confusedly, Pip has felt guilt about the attack on Mrs Joe: he knows he didn't do it but that the worst part of him may have wanted to: Orlick is here allowed to articulate this barely conscious fear. And his epitaph, an invention not of Dickens but of the screenplay, is spoken by Pip, who, by this time, has begun to understand the needs and frustrations of others.

4 Grahame Smith, *Dickens and the Dream of Cinema*. Manchester and New York: Manchester University Press, 2003, p. 13.

As for those other young(ish) men, the parish clerk Wopsle (Peter Benson) is shown as accompanying Joe and Pip with the soldiers to look for the convicts, thus separating him from Pumblechook and Hubble, who, through cowardice or greater age, stay at the forge. In this small detail, the mini-series prepares us for the Wopsle who is bold enough to leave the village, where he is renowned for his grandiloquent way with the 'Amens', to make his way to London as an actor, now called Waldengraver. The church's loss seems unlikely to be the theatre's gain, but he is here presented as an oblique reflection of Pip, as another villager trying his luck in the big city and this screenplay gives him his moment. Contrasted with Pip who is an ungrateful 'son' to Joe until his other 'father', Magwitch, gives him a second chance at the filial, Wemmick (Colin Jeavons[5]) is a model son who is contented with his lot in life, grateful to his inane and deaf Aged Parent (Tony Sympson) whom he treats with unerring solicitude. Wemmick has significantly needed to keep his fanciful but wholesome family life separate from the contagion of contact with the milieu of Little Britain and Newgate, whereas Pip has been unable to keep his aspirations and his other feelings so conveniently separate.

Most compelling among these figures who in their various ways offer distorting parallels with Pip (and one is surprised that that other *contented* provincial, Trabb's boy, is no more than a name in this comprehensive adaptation) is that of Herbert Pocket. Apart from Joe, to whom Pip stands, as noted, almost in the position of a son, Herbert is Pip's first real friend, and in this version their friendship is treated with an expansiveness not found elsewhere, and that includes even the charming performance of Alec Guinness in

---

[5] Jeavons had played Herbert in the 1959 mini-series, and Richard Carstone in the first TV version of *Bleak House* in the same year.

Lean's film. The relationship between Pip and Herbert here becomes one of the major 'positives' of the tale. Herbert (Tim Munro) is a young man with no expectations: he has failed to impress Miss Havisham and his father can't help him. He is in love with Clara (Melanie Hughes) whose station is well below his foolish mother's aristocratic fantasies, and the friendship that grows between him and Pip derives partly from their willingness to confide their yearnings to each other. Though the scene in which Herbert tells Pip the story of Miss Havisham's blighted hopes and, in turn, how his father and he have no hopes of her helping them, is too long and expository, the film builds the friendship between the two young men so convincingly that their final parting is unexpectedly very touching. In Herbert, Pip has found a real live sibling to replace those who went untimely to their graves.

This 1981 version has several other distinctions, as well as its insightful dealings with young men making what they can from the material of their lives. It exhibits throughout careful production design (the work of Michael Edwards): Satis House persuasively evokes not just desuetude but *wealth* in desuetude; Pip and Herbert's rooms become subtly more comfortable as Pip gets into the swing of spending his generous allowance; Wemmick's 'castle' has an aptly eccentric charm; and so on. Further, the colour photography differentiates effectively between, say, the bleakness of the marshes and forge, all in muted browns, and the faintly eerie blue light of the Satis House interiors. In the matter of costume, the beauty of the grown Estella (Sarah-Jane Varley) is set off and made to seem more unattainable by the brilliance of magenta, royal blue and dazzling white in the ballroom. My point is that this is a handsome production but that physical aspects, such as the foregoing, are not allowed to overwhelm the central drama of aspiration and guilt and, in Miss Havisham's phrase, 'abject devotion'.

Mention of Miss Havisham leads one to note that this is an extremely well acted version of the novel. The role of Miss Havisham, so central to our understanding of Pip's motivation, however wrong his suppositions, has attracted uniformly fine performances. Even in such inferior films as the 1934 and 1975 versions, there were rewards in the acting of, respectively, Florence Reed and Margaret Leighton. In the 1981 version she is given an outstandingly acute reading from Joan Hickson. Best known as TV's Miss Marple in the 1980s, Hickson was in fact a remarkable actress and here, avoiding mere eccentricity, intuits and conveys Miss Havisham's bitterly won knowledge of the darker aspects of human behaviour. On the occasion of Pip's final visit to her, she has a way of sitting and staring that bespeak the utter futility and waste of her life, and there is pathos as she weeps on 'What have I done?' As well there is a fine Joe from Philip Joseph, a simple, good man and not at all a fool, and Derek Francis's Jaggers is allowed a moment of human compassion as he talks of what was done to save the child Estella. Sundquist's Pip gathers authority as he deals with the business of saving Magwitch and of his own redemption and Sarah-Jane Varley's Estella, recalling Valerie Hobson in Lean's film, has a clear, taunting beauty and hauteur, which, as noted above, her costumes underscore.

Julian Amyes, an ex-actor,[6] may not have set out to make a startling reworking of the text, but, despite sometimes allowing a too-leisurely pace, he unobtrusively achieves some subtly alert effects. For example, with the help of his editor, he neatly juxtaposes Pip's view of Mrs Joe's prone body with the sound of the cannon from the prison hulk, initiating in him that frisson of guilt to which Orlick will later snarlingly refer – and one remembers this earlier

[6] He has supporting roles in such films as *High Treason* (1951) and *Mandy* (1952).

echo at that later moment. Or the tiny touches of childish malice in the young Estella, smiling meanly at Joe's awkwardness when he visits Satis House, or the shot of the flowers Pip has brought her, later seen lying dead on the floor where she has thrown them (did Alfonso Cuarón remember this image when he made his film version in 1997?). In a more clearly important matter, there is a telling contrast between Jaggers' inscrutable complexity and Joe's open simplicity that the film enforces in contrasting stances and facial expression.

It would be a mistake to overpraise this essentially workmanlike adaptation but equally we should acknowledge the thoroughness with which it is steeped in Dickens, to recognise that it sometimes casts an unexpected light on familiar things and that it ends by being movingly aware of the costs of loving and living and of the rewards open to those who have learnt enough to appreciate them. The final sentence of the novel is spoken by Pip in voice-over and he is last seen standing by the gibbet on the marshes: in the decision to end in this way are encapsulated the twin strands of Amyes' production: its closeness to the letter of the novel and its quiet way of stamping it with something new.

Great Expectations (1999)
Director: Julian Jarrold; screenplay Tony Marchand

By comparison with the 1981 version, this, at 180 minutes, is a streamlined version of the novel, and the difference in the two running times points to a distinction in the respective treatments of the original. Again, like the earlier mini-series, this reveals a more or less even division of running-time among the three 'stages' of the story, unlike the cinema films which to date have always favoured the earlier stage in which the key influences on Pip's development are set in place. Jarrold's version, though, from Tony Marchand's screenplay, offers a decidedly more idiosyncratic response to the 'hypotext', to use Gérard Genette's term.[7]

Increasingly, in considering adaptations of *Great Expectations* of the last fifty or sixty years, one feels that 'hypotext' includes not just Dickens but significantly as well the David Lean film of 1946. This comes to mind particularly in relation to Jarrold's version which seems to announce from the beginning its intention not to be read as yet another remake. Unlike virtually every other adaptation of the novel, it does not begin with Pip in the churchyard on a gloomy winter afternoon, with wind sighing and boughs creaking in proleptic terror of the confrontation we are all waiting for. Instead, it opens on a medium long shot of waving corn, with a small boy emerging above it, then running wildly through it to a graveyard where he falls behind a tombstone, cowering as the shackled legs of (we assume) a convict appear to stand over him. The credits then unfold over the muted landscape of the marshlands and the film cuts to the Gargery kitchen, where Mrs Joe, a truly vicious harridan, belabours him and an ineffectual Joe tries to comfort him. Only when he is later in bed does he recall the encounter with Magwitch (an alarming ruffian in Bernard Hill's interpretation): this is mostly shot in close-up as Magwitch shakes Pip, then turns him upside down. The film then cuts to Pip stealing brandy, then to a close-up of the tar-water bottle, and then to a long shot as he runs through the mist, emerging from the evocatively ghostly forms of the trees. There is no sign of Compeyson, but as Magwitch wolfs down the food Pip has brought he mentions almost in passing that 'Compeyson is out'. This reversal of the order of the novel – the details of the original graveyard encounter only being recalled

[7] Gérard Genette, *Palimpsestes: La Littérature au second degré*. Paris: Editions du Seuil, 1982, p. 13.

later – is presumably Jarrold's way of assuring us that what we will see *is* Pip's story, that this is how he has remembered it. In another startling break, not just with Dickens and Lean but with the whole tradition relating to the filming of this novel, Marchant's screenplay will largely eschew the first-person voice-over, so that Pip's relation to the events must make itself felt in other ways.

The great influences on Pip's early life are all represented in ways that suggest a conscious re-imagining on the part of Jarrold and Marchant. This Joe (Clive Russell), can be pushed too far, and he can be rough, as though the effort of dealing with so mean-spirited a wife has had an effect even on one so innately good. As you observe Lesley Sharp's riveting performance as Mrs Joe – a feminist's view of a woman imploding with rage at the limitations of her life – you also understand that Joe's goodness can only have been maintained at the cost of suppressing *his* feelings about her. One writer described her, accurately, in this performance as 'a simmering bomb ever ready to explode. And for once, we began to understand what a bum hand life had dealt her'.[8] We are made to feel for her sense of exclusion when Miss Havisham asks for Joe to visit but with no word of invitation for his wife; and, while Pip may be about to be taken up by the rich recluse, she, Mrs Joe, is condemned to the lot of blacksmith's wife. There is a real snarling nastiness in her reaction here, but the screenplay and the actress enable us to see where it has come from. Joe, in turn and perhaps in consequence, is a less substantial figure in this adaptation, and deprived of the novel's scene in which he comes to London, to Pip's embarrassment and his own discomfort, he emerges much less sympathetically than usual.

[8] Robert Giddings, *'Great Expectations'*, *The Dickensian*.
See http://charlesdickenspage.com/great_expectations_giddings.html

The Miss Havisham of Jarrold's version is, in Charlotte Rampling's elegantly understated performance, younger, more beautiful, less ravaged and less mad than most of the other interpreters of the role. She is still handsome and intelligent enough to make us aware of what a blow to her self-esteem the jilting must have been. There is a more refined cruelty at work in her than we are used to, and there is the sense of an amused collusion between her and the young Estella, a more modern child who pushes Pumblechook back outside the gate, but one in whom the heartless chill is not yet fully in place. There is a feminist element in the reworking of Miss Havisham here: far from Martita Hunt's wonderful grotesque, this is a woman of wealth, as the production design makes clear, a woman of distinction and perhaps of humour – a woman, that is, who might reasonably have expected a great deal more of life than to be cruelly passed over. Nothing in Rampling's taut control asks for sympathy; as a result, this Miss Havisham excites pity.

The other two who will so affect the course of Pip's life – Magwitch and Jaggers – are incisively portrayed by actors who seem also to have shaken off the mantle of their forebears in the Lean film. Bernard Hill's Magwitch is a violent angry man to whom the later benignity does not come easily. When he returns from Australia to find his 'gentleman', he is rougher, more knowing, more insinuating, more alarming than the farouche dignity of Finlay Currie's performance in Lean's film could have suggested, and one understands fully Pip's recoil from this revenant, who excites not only his fear for his safety but also the collapse of his hopes regarding Estella. In a curious touch, this Magwitch, having created his gentleman, is not altogether sure that he can trust him. Jaggers, as played by Ian McDiarmid, is even more surprising. He does not appear in the film until he comes to the forge with the eponymous news for Pip, so that the connection with Miss Havisham is not hinted at, and, as if determined to come out from under the long shadow cast by Francis L. Sullivan's two incarnations of Jaggers in the 1934 and 1946 films, McDiarmid offers a quieter, sharper Jaggers, a Jaggers in whom the repeated hand-washing retains its metonymic functions. Here, though, it seems more than just an unconscious attempt to rid himself of the ugly associations of his profession; there is as well a hint of neurotic compulsion at work in this seemingly self-contained man.

The television mini-series very often seems to be more a writer's medium than a director's. Is there, for instance, a director whose name is so tenaciously associated with the genre as writer Andrew Davies' name is? Here, though, I should want to argue as much for the direction of Julian Jarrold as for Tony Marchant's screenplay: together they have fashioned from Dickens a fable for the late twentieth century. In large matters, such as class and gender distinctions, the film offers a way of reading the novel that was not available to its first readers, and I shall return to this. In particular, local matters of the film-maker's art and craft, Jarrold stamps the film as his own: he seems in this way to be something more individual than a merely careful *metteur-en-scène* or impersonal craftsman. One of his most striking stylistic tropes is his use of extreme close-ups of things as well as people to focus attention, again metonymically, on a narrative element. The cards which the young Pip and Estella play with at Satis House and over which he shames himself by calling the knaves 'jacks' are seen first in the close-up that motivates her scornful remark. Years later when Pip goes to visit Miss Havisham, despite Joe's warning against this, the camera lingers fleetingly on the same pack of cards, as if to recall to him the shame he'd once felt because of them. There is also an insistent use of close-up images of hands which seems peculiarly apt in the unfolding of a narrative in which 'manipulation' of young lives is so crucial. Miss Havisham's hand, most manipulative of all, is extended for Pip to kiss as he leaves for London, and that same hand will be all we see of her burnt body, over which this Pip will weep. There are of course close-ups of Jaggers' hands as he washes them and of the enigmatic Molly's wrists. Finally, there is a poignant close-up of Pip's hand holding Magwitch's in the prison infirmary, a gesture expressing some reconciliation in Pip with the past, literally with the convict whose hands had grasped and shaken him when he was a frightened child. As to faces, the Christmas dinner scene, with all its idiotic conversation, most of it directed at Pip's youthful ingratitude, is conducted almost entirely in close-ups, alternating between the faces of the foolish speakers and their victim. This combination is echoed in the close-up in which Pip's ever more baroque lies about Satis House are told and received. And most striking, the briefly held close-up of Pip's face, lit so as to distinguish him from the surrounding darkness, is just enough to assure Magwitch that Pip hasn't betrayed him. In a subtle touch, the boy Pip gets an upside down reflection of his face in a bucket of water which recalls the close-up of his face as he remembers how the convict had upended him.

By contrast, the occasional long shot makes its point: the marshes and the forge in their bleakness are held in an unusually long take when Pip rides off with Pumblechook on his first visit to Satis House, as if to underline the significance of this break with all he might have expected of life. The marshes offer no refuge for Pip, either at this early stage or later when he fights in the open with Orlick (Tony Curran). Dickens was never sentimental about rural or village life, and when he was tempted to paint a rosy picture of rural retreat, as in parts of *Oliver Twist*, sentimentality was the result; the labyrinth of the city fascinated even when it repelled him; and the long shots of Satis House may mean harm to Pip, but, as the camera cuts back to the forge, it is clear that there is no comfort to be found *there*, nor in a London introduced by blood in the streets, emanating from the carcasses of Smithfield. Whichever way Pip turns, there does not seem much prospect for joy.

I have spent time in referring to these points of style because they are not usually found in discussions of television adaptations, as if the whole job of the adaptors was to satisfy the expectations of 'the centrally minority bourgeois audience of BBC 2' as David Lusted has diagnosed.[9] My argument is that these stylistic characteristics are indicators of the film-maker's purchase on his material. This purchase is of course to be found in other – thematic – ways, involving the highlighting of this or that aspect of the novel to provide a new emphasis. In this case, the way the women are represented is perhaps the most compelling and original facet of Jarrold and Marchant's adaptation. That there is some understanding of the woman lurking beneath the virago in the case of Mrs Joe, of the wounded vanity beneath the apparent eccentric reclusivity of Miss Havisham, has been touched on. The interest in the damaged lives of women does not end there. Estella's marriage to the egregious Bentley Drummle ends in disaster. She has married him despite Pip's passionate plea to her not to 'give yourself away to that stupid brute' and some time – and five sequences – later there is a brief glimpse of the bruised Estella standing in the window of Drummle's house. The damage to her has been physical, adding to the psychological damage done her by her guardian's policy of training her to seek vengeance on the male sex. And finally, Molly (Laila Morse). She is quite unusually

9 David Lusted, 'Literary adaptations and cultural fantasies', *Journal of Popular British Cinema*, No. 4, 2001, p. 77.

treated in this version. When first seen in Jaggers' house when he has invited Pip and others to dinner, she surprises by asking Pip about Satis House. A little later, when Estella arrives in London, vivid in a bright red dress as the square empties while she waits for Pip to meet her, she is observed by Molly whose overhead shot of the solitary girl we share. Molly, Estella's mother, is another woman who has been harmed by the men she has been in contact with. The foregoing is not sufficient to label this a 'feminist' version of the novel but it does indicate a persistent strand via which Jarrold has put his director's mark on the material.

At the centre of the action is of course Pip, and in this case there is an unusually convincing likeness between the actors who play him as a boy (Gabriel Thomson) and as a young man (Ioan Gruffudd). This ensures a continuity of interest in the protagonist and because there is no voice-over the film relies more than ordinarily on our involvement with Pip. The matter of close-ups discussed above is one way in which Pip's point of view is put before us: they are almost invariably as seen by Pip. Sometimes, too, what might have been voice-over commentary – that is, elements of the novel's discursive, first-person prose – is delivered by Pip as direct speech, as when he talks to Biddy about Estella, saying: 'Sometimes she tells me energetically that she hates me', an observation that is part of Pip's continuing reflection on the action in the novel. Pip's centrality is confirmed, not only in the handsome Gruffudd's strong and varied performance, but in his relations with the other young men in the story, notably Orlick and Herbert. The friendship with Herbert (Daniel Evans) is still a strongly positive note in his development, without its acquiring the forceful poignancy of Amyes' 1981 version. The contrast with Orlick is achieved with a brief complexity that is hinted at but not developed in the 1981 version. One of the most potent episodes in Jarrold's version is the fight between Orlick and Pip, here taking place out in the open on the marshes. Orlick's grievances – he is the journeyman blacksmith's apprentice who never had a stroke of good fortune – are given an airing that compels our attention. 'And now you're a gentleman and I can't get a living,' he (perhaps justly) complains. Pip explains, his life being at stake, that his benefactor is a convict and that the woman he loves is married to someone else. Orlick then, in a very interesting, idiosyncratic moment of interpretation, lets him go, saying: 'I am more than your equal. I let you go.' This use of Orlick as a sort of *alter ego* for Pip, the basis for which is surely there in Dickens, is one of the distinguishing marks of this adaptation. There is too a strongly sensual bond signified between Pip and Justine Waddell's cold repressed Estella, combining as she does, in Giddings' phrase, 'exactly the right proportions of sexual magnetism and emotional paralysis.'[10]

This is – as television adaptations go – a mini-series with a strong visual sense. Original touches in interpretation, at least original in the light of most preceding versions, are articulated in no small measure through Jarrold's command of his medium. He makes it do the work of narrative rather than simply dealing with the events of the hypotext and engaging in a filming-by-numbers process. Though the montage which enacts Pip's education as a gentleman may recall a similar filmic treatment of this series of activities in Lean's film, Jarrold and Marchant have elsewhere made something new of the central tale of aspiration, education and reclamation. They have been much more cavalier than some other adaptors in relation to the cardinal functions listed earlier in this book (omitting Joe's London visit is a crucial example of what I mean), and they arrive at a different end point. Lusted is surely absolutely right in his reading

---

[10] Giddings, op cit.

of the last moments of this version. There is no suggestion that the old confining class barriers have been torn down. Pip and Estella are in Satis House certainly, but this Pip doesn't rip away the rotten curtains to let in the light of a freer, more equitable society. No, he joins Estella who has settled there and 'made many changes in the way of decoration'. Pip bitterly anticipates her future there, but succumbs to an embrace and to a recognition that both have suffered. 'Do we have to part again because we cannot act on our love for each other?' he asks, and they settle to playing cards. 'Is that a knave or a jack?' he asks, as the camera pulls further and further back to reveal them together at the table. As Lusted says of this camera movement, 'they become more and more trapped together, victims of an inescapable past.'[11] Unlike in 1946 when it might have been possible to predict, or at least to hope for, a brave new democratic world, by 1999 it has clearly not happened and Jarrold's adaptation of Dickens reflects not just the anterior text but the climate in which he is making his film. It is not just a matter of 'the superficial similarities between the television serial and Dickens' publication of his novels in instalments' that is at issue here, but a shared 'ambition of vision and a willingness to take the social and moral temperature of the nation'[12] What angered Dickens, seemed hopeful to Lean in 1946, now seems to be a matter of atrophy to Jarrold and Marchant in 1999.

Conclusion

It is worth looking carefully at these two television adaptations both for their considerable intrinsic merits and for the ways in which they encourage us to see new things in their rich antecedent literary

 [11] Lusted, op cit.

[12] Ray Cathode, 'Rising damp', *Sight and Sound*, March 1999, p. 33.

text. In their diverse ways, they both draw on the great strengths of the novel, on the vividness of its characters and their complex interconnections, on the powerfully influential effect that adults with an agenda may have on the young, on the contrasting circumstances that shape the adults we become. They also make us aware of how so great a novel can inspire such divergent responses, can fix the attention of film-makers on such different aspects of the precursor text. Have we ever before, for instance, seen a Mrs Joe so full of class rage? In both such detail and in over-arching interpretation, these two television versions have a lot to offer in what they have found in Dickens and in the way their own different social attitudes have shaded their reading.

great expectations (1934): a hollywood studio romance

··

Perhaps the most interesting thing about Stuart Walker's 1934 version of the novel for Universal Studios is that, while for maybe three-quarters of its length it follows the main events and even reproduces much of the dialogue of the original, it never begins to *feel* like the original. It is not only lacking in the powerful atmospheric influences at work in Dickens's story; it singularly fails to create its own sense of any darker forces at work in the lives of its young protagonists. What emerges finally is bland romance in which the potential for serious conflict is smoothed away and the whole has the look of a nicely-lit, prettily-set studio production. Odd moments suddenly surprise us with touches of poignancy or unexpected sharpness in the playing, but these are few and far between in what amounts to a filming-by-numbers exercise for much of the time, with a conventional, toothless Hollywood resolution at the end.

Narrative events

As noted previously, Dickens divided *Great Expectations* into three almost equal 'stages', the 'first stage' of 'Pip's expectations' coming as he leaves the village bound for London and the 'second stage' as he is left stunned by Magwitch's return. The 1934 film adheres very closely to the main narrative events of the first third of the novel, deals sluggishly with the material of the second stage, and gallops over the third. It is as though director and screenwriter Gladys Unger (who worked with Walker the following year on the film version of Dickens's unfinished novel, *The Mystery of Edwin Drood*) were more comfortable with the swift movement of events rather than with the inner drama of Pip's moral growth and reclamation. But even at this level, the film works more like a simplified illustration of the original text than a re-imagining of it.

With superior film versions of the novel in our mind (superior both as films in their own right and as adaptations), it is now not easy to place oneself in the 1934 viewing context for Walker's film. It opens, as we would expect, in the graveyard, very clearly a studio set, and the young Pip, played by George P. Breakston as a familiarly `cute' American kid, is talking to the gravestones of his late parents and brothers, picking up the cue from the novel's opening paragraph about his childish imaginings on the subject of his family's headstones. The narrative moves quickly with the sudden appearance of Magwitch the convict (there are several good, alarming closeups of Henry Hull in this role), who threatens Pip with talk of a terrible `young man' and orders him to bring food and file.

The events and much of the dialogue of most of the first half of the film are taken directly from the novel. In Roland Barthes' terms,[1] the `cardinal functions' of narrative, those `hinge-points' or `risky moments' of narrative which open up the possibility of alternative consequences for the plot's further development, are transferred

---

[1] Roland Barthes, `Introduction to the Structural Analysis of Narratives' (1966), in *Image-Music-Text*, trans. Stephen Heath. Glasgow: Fontana/Collins, 1977, p. 93.

from the novel.[2] When Magwitch appears, he may or may not harm Pip; Pip may or may not carry out Magwitch's instructions; he steals the food and the file for Magwitch, and we wonder what Magwitch's response will be. And so on. The transferring of actual events from page to screen is no guarantee of creating a comparable atmosphere or of the characters involved affecting us in the same way as they did on the page. It is one thing to 'transfer' an incident, whether a crucial one with serious possible consequences or a minor one (e.g., 'Mrs Joe scrubs Pip roughly'); it is another to take up notations of atmosphere or mood or character and to try to recreate these in another medium, another semiotic system which uses audio-visual moving images, not merely words on a page. To do this, supposing the film-maker is interested in reproducing such intangibles, requires what I would call processes of 'adaptation proper' as distinct from those of transfer.[3]

Walker's 1934 film reveals very little interest in the building up of either the kind of atmosphere of gloom and fear that is there in the opening of the novel or of the wit that accompanies the mature Pip's account of these events. This is not to say that nothing is worth noting but that the pleasures are incidental, not seeming to derive from any coherent sense of what the narrative *means*. The notion of a young life's being randomly wrenched out of its course with the potential for wide-ranging effect on the course of his development is scarcely hinted at, so that we are left with events following each other more or less as they do in the novel but without the novel's – or anyone else's – sense of their significance. One notes

[2] Barthes' classification of narrative functions underpins my theory of adaptation and my use of it is discussed in my book, *Novel to Film: An Introduction to the Theory of Adaptation*. Oxford: Clarendon Press, OUP, 1996, pp. 13ff.
[3] Ibid., pp. 23–26 re 'transfer' and pp. 26–27 re 'adaptation proper'.

in passing that Mrs Joe as played by Rafaela Ottiano has a touch of the true virago, that the fight between Magwitch and the other convict is shot with vivid use of overhead shots and close-ups, and that the unexpectedness of the life of Satis House beyond the decaying bridal room strikes us as realistic (that is, the occupants don't live their days entirely among the cobwebby decay of the bridal-banquet room).

Shifting structures

As I write this, I am aware of trying conscientiously (but not neces-sarily succeeding) to put from my mind later, more carefully made versions of *Great Expectations*, which show up the perfunctoriness of much of this earlier film. It is not just a matter of this being an old, studio-made film: George Cukor's rousing, large-spirited *David Copperfield* (1934) and Jack Conway's *A Tale of Two Cities* (1935) show what could be achieved in not dissimilar production circum-stances in the same era: rather, it is a matter of the film's lacking a coherent vision or any sort of style that would make the events mean something serious about the thwarting of young lives. Also, the film is, as I suggested above, curiously unbalanced, in compari-son with the novel at least, in its dealings with the stages of Pip's fortunes. By this I mean that it takes 49 minutes to deal with Pip's career up to the point of his leaving the village for London, 35 minutes to chronicle his London life and the disruptive return of Magwitch, and a mere 19 minutes to record the drama of Pip's moral reclamation.

This is not to berate the film-makers for not adhering to Dickens's structure, but for not finding a significant structure of their own. In adapting the first third of the novel, Walker moves smoothly if unexcitingly through the novel's major cardinal functions – the meeting with Magwitch, Magwitch's capture, Pip's visit to Miss

Havisham and meeting with and falling in love with Estella, Jaggers' bringing news of Pip's 'great expectations', and Pip's farewell to Miss Havisham whom he believes to be his benefactor. The material contained in the second third of the novel is much more compressed. The film-makers are not much interested in Pip's social education: this is limited to a couple of polite tips from Herbert Pocket and a very brief scene in which he is outfitted as a gentleman; and there is almost no sense of the effect of his London life on him. Compare this with his growing snobbery and extravagance in the novel: again, this is not a complaint growing out of a misguided notion of 'fidelity', but, rather, a wish that the events might *mean* something. In the long sequence in which Magwitch returns to London, there is a briefly vivid image as he stretches his arms out to Pip in a gesture that echoes his cruciform posture against a headstone in the graveyard when he is waiting for Pip with the food. After this imaginative touch connecting the convict to Pip's childhood encounter, the episode drags on with a great deal of expository dialogue and a flashback relating to Magwitch's meeting with Molly, the birth of their daughter and the association with the other convict, Compeyson. This account takes a chapter in the novel too, but there it is vivified by the consistency of Magwitch's voice. Following this long, slow, stagy episode, Walker brings the film towards its rushed conclusion. Both Pip and Estella reproach Miss Havisham, for respectively misleading and misteaching them; Estella plans to marry the boorish Bentley Drummle; Pip confronts Jaggers with knowledge of Magwitch's return and revelations; an aborted attempt to save Magwitch leads to his recapture, trial and death in prison; and Pip and Estella are suddenly reunited.

Shifts in emphasis

Given this structure, what are the effects on the nature of the adaptation? For instance, how far do the influences that govern Pip's development survive? The film presents him in a somewhat milder version of the child-as-victim: he is still the victim of the convict's threats, of Mrs Joe's bullying, of Miss Havisham's vengeance on the male sex and of Estella's snobbish disdain for his being 'a common labouring boy'. We can see the traces of this sort of pattern of influence, though the impact of them is flattened by the film's lack of narrative rhythm, which leads to a placidity of unfolding without much in the way of contrast or heightening in the interests of drama. By lack of contrast I chiefly mean that the figure of Joe (played by Alan Hale) is very much diminished in this film and Biddy does not appear in the film at all,[4] so that there's nothing to balance those whose aim it is to make Pip's life more difficult.

In the section of film devoted to rendering the novel's 'second stage', there is very little interest in Pip's development. His 'education' as a gentleman is virtually omitted as noted above; the effects of his arbitrary rise in social status are non-existent. Could it be that Hollywood in 1934 couldn't conceive of a hero so susceptible to unworthy snobberies? In any event, the crucial visit of Joe to London, in which Pip realises that he has become a snob, is missing and, indeed, Joe is never seen again after Pip leaves his village to go to London. In Joe's absence, there is no figure against whom we might have assessed Pip's moral progress, even if the film had been interested in this. The rivalry between Pip and the

---

[4] Valerie Hobson is listed in the cast at the end of the film but her scenes were deleted. In fact, she went to Hollywood to play Estella, but, at 17, was deemed too young for the part and given Biddy as compensation. She would, of course, play Estella in David Lean's 1946 version. Interview with author, June 1990.

repellent Drummle over Estella loses both the social element and the strange power of Estella having been trained to have 'no heart' and is little more than commonplace triangle fiction. Though Estella warns Pip against loving her in the ballroom scene, their romance, both at this point and elsewhere (especially at the end), is treated in utterly conventional terms, most often accompanied by a sugary score. The return of Magwitch, which is the turning point in the novel for Pip's fortunes and the beginning of his moral reclamation, is given due weight in terms of running-time, but there's been no pattern of childish guilt or the guilt of shame about his origins to which it might have provided the climax. It remains a plot function rather than a key moment in thematic terms.

As to the final 'stage', the film collapses the matter of the novel into a rushed business of Estella's confrontation of Miss Havisham, of Pip's trying to effect Magwitch's escape, and of the final embrace of Pip and Estella, Magwitch now dead and Estella disengaged from Drummle. The speed and conventionality of this section of the film robs it of any resonance. The drama of Pip's growth in moral understanding and stature as he accepts the source of his expectations and seeks to help Magwitch passes for little and the time he spends at Magwitch's deathbed loses most of the pathos it might have had if the film had been interested in the processes by which Pip has been transformed from idle young 'gentleman' to one capable of such unselfish feeling. His inability in a moment of the film's invention to write 'I forgive her' in Miss Havisham's Bible is potentially interesting but is too fleeting to register much. It is interesting too as a contradiction of the situation in the novel and suggests a hard-edged perception that might have been rewarding to pursue. The romantic dénouement, perhaps true to an early 1930s Hollywood, mirroring a world emerging from a major depression, is utterly perfunctory and conventionally sentimental.

Instead of the novel's harsh account of Drummle's breaking his engagement to Estella when he discovers her parentage, we are offered the softer idea of Estella as initiating the break because of love for Pip.

Is it Dickensian?

To ask this question is not to imply that this is necessarily a major aim of an adaptation of *Great Expectations*; it is however one way of coming to terms with the sort of film that has been made. Universal was not a studio much committed either to period films or to luxurious production values. Compared with MGM's much more lavish version of *David Copperfield* or *The Barretts of Wimpole Street*, released in the same year, or with Fox's *Cavalcade* (1933), or even with Universal's *Frankenstein* (1932) or *The Invisible Man* (1933), Walker's film version of *Great Expectations* is singularly lacking in any feel for (Victorian) England or for the flamboyance of Dickens. This is largely a matter of production design and this film is obviously studio-bound: even episodes that are meant to be taking place out of doors (e.g., the graveyard opening; the failed escape on the river) have a distinctly studio look, in contrast with some of the later versions, made at a time when location work was more common film-making practice. The sets in the 1934 film are no more than adequate. They don't sufficiently distinguish among the various social classes represented in, say, the Gargery house, Satis House or Jaggers' London establishment. Street scenes, such as that in which Estella arrives at the London coachyard, suggest a romanticised Christmas-card version of the city, rather than Pip's initial 'doubts whether it was not rather ugly, crooked, narrow, and dirty' (Ch. XX). The codes of *mise-en-scène*, involving here décor, lighting, costume and camera-placement are truer to 1934 Hollywood than to nineteenth-century Britain.

As to the acting there are some major deficiencies, though this of course is always a subjective matter. The young Pip and Estella are played as standard Hollywood children of the period – he as a regular Jackie Coogan-ish lad, she as a pouty little miss. When they grow up, they become little more than a pair of pretty puppets in the performances of Phillips Holmes and Jane Wyatt, though not actually conveying the aspect of puppets (the strings pulled by various adults including Magwitch, Miss Havisham and Jaggers) that might have been true to their characters. We feel particularly the diminution of the character of Pip who is one of Dickens's most fully realised heroes. The absence of Trabb's boy and Orlick as two provincial young men who don't inherit property and who are subsequently, in the novel, made the objects of Pip's superior denunciations, the thinning-down of Herbert Pockel's kindly optimism, the reducing of Drummle to a briefly glimpsed dinner-guest and dance-partner, and above all the relegation of Joe to the opening episodes: these gaps and etiolations mean that there is not much left for us to measure Pip against. As for Estella, she is perhaps no more than an idea in Dickens – the concept of one educated to feel nothing – but even she lacks the contrasting warmth of Biddy to help us to understand her inner chill. In the end, these two are no more than stereotyped romantic leads, fighting a losing battle against banal dialogue and a syrupy musical soundtrack.

Pip is no doubt a difficult role. The actor has to enlist our interest in the character who is clearly the protagonist, yet is by comparison with the grotesques who surround him a somewhat pallid figure. We must be made interested in his development and the processes of his moral renewal if he is to hold attention alongside the vivid likes of Miss Havisham, Magwitch and others. In this film, as suggested above, Phillips Holmes is allowed to be no more than a mildly good-looking leading man, but it is not necessarily because he is overshadowed by the supporting gargoyles that it is difficult to take his situation seriously. To turn to these latter, not merely in fact 'gargoyles' but in Propp's terminology, a series of figures who, irrespective of the 'completely distinctive, vivid colouring'[5] they may add, crucially perform such character *functions* as 'villain', 'helper' and others in relation to the 'hero'. Given the element of fairy-tale in the story of Pip's humble origins, rise to fortune, disillusionment and final growth to a more stable maturity, these characters assume a significance more than that of mere entertainment. Indeed, Pip sees himself, erroneously as it happens, as marked out to 'do all the shining deeds of the young Knight of romance, and marry the Princess' (Ch. XXIX). The very use of capitals seems to lead us to a Proppian reading of the main line of the novel's narrative.

In this film, however, the strong character functions which Dickens attributes to these people are vitiated by either under-exposure, misplaced realism or staginess. Joe, as indicated already, plays no part in his redemption and is reduced to a few early scenes of good-natured bewilderment. There are some moments of pathos from former silent-screen star Florence Reed as Miss Havisham, created in terms less eccentrically memorable than Martita Hunt's incarnation in 1946 but with some poignancy in her depiction of ruined hopes and cold revenge. Henry Hull's Magwitch has a theatrical intensity and orotund delivery that are apt to be at odds with the film's generally low-key realism, though 'realism' may not be the term that later generations would apply to the film's mode. Most interesting is the British actor Francis L. Sullivan's Jaggers, which in hindsight seems like a preliminary sketch

[5] V. Propp, *Morphology of the Folktale* (1927), trans. Laurence Scott. Austin: University of Texas, 1968, p. 21.

for his definitive 1946 representation of the same role. In this earlier film, there is a credible suggestion of perceptive humanity in his account to Pip of the role he has played in Estella's adoption. Wemmick and his Aged P. are missing altogether and Pumble-chook, Wopsle and others are barely glimpsed, but such omissions and near-omissions do not constitute necessary grounds for complaint: it may well be more satisfactory to reduce the cast list of so populous a novel than to try to include them all without giving them anything worth doing.

One of the few accounts of the film, and a brief one at that, allows that, though Walker's film failed to 'capture the essential essence' (*sic*), 'it diligently covered most of the narrative highlights of the novel'.[6] This is at least arguable, despite the rushed final movement of the film, but that tautology about 'essential essence' perhaps gestures towards the way the film fails on a thematic level. Up to a point it reproduces in the cinema's semiotic system the main events of a good part of the novel, but in those matters less susceptible to transfer, matters having to do with what Barthes would call 'integrational' functions[7] – notations of character, of tone, of atmosphere – the film has little in common with the anterior text. The *Bildungsroman* element loses a good deal of its potency as a result of Pip's being deprived of the comparative characters of Trabb's boy and Orlick, of the sense of powerful moral influence exerted by Joe (sensitivity in his treatment of Joe is a key factor in Pip's redemption), or of the sense of mysterious influence in the characters of Magwitch and Miss Havisham (the one over-, the other under-played, in terms of their chief character functions). As a result Pip's moral slackening and subsequent redemption are

[6] Clive Hirschhorn, *The Universal Story*. London: Octopus Books, 1983, p. 84.
[7] Barthes, op cit, p. 92.

scarcely registered as such, and we are left pretty much with a love story that runs into a few obstacles.

It would not be worth labouring this film if it were not to make the point that a conscientious attention to the events of a novel, and even to its dialogue, is no guarantee either of evoking the thematic interests of the original or of creating a film with its own thematic agenda.

great expectations (1975): a musical sans songs

From the moment the credits come up on a royal blue satin background, against which the chief actors/characters appear individually in oval frames, mostly addressing the camera, we are aware of a kind of fake 'quality' approach to this enterprise. The four faces before the title are those of Michael York (Pip), Sarah Miles (Estella), James Mason (Magwich) and Robert Morley (Pumblechook). There are two things we might note about this line-up: for some reason Dickens's Magwitch has lost his 't' (did the film-makers just misread?), and Morley's star clout was presumably enough to ensure the minor character of Pumblechook gets pre-credit billing whereas, say, Margaret Leighton (Miss Havisham) and Anthony Quayle (Jaggers) only appear after the title. Further, there is a generally smiling, confiding look about all these faces presented to us before the story begins. Nothing about this intro-ductory material seems to bode well for an adaptation of one of Dickens's most sombre, complex and demanding novels, at least not for viewers who want to see those qualities preserved in this filmed re-telling.

The film is shot in Panavision by triple Oscar-winner Freddie Young; the music is by another triple Oscar-winner, Maurice Jarre, who, like Young, had been much associated with David Lean in his epic mode; there is an undoubtedly distinguished cast; and costumes are by Elizabeth Haffenden and Joan Bridge. In other words, the television director, Joseph Hardy, has surrounded himself with what must have seemed like fail-proof collaborators in this production for Transcontinental Films and Lew Grade's ITC. The production context includes two factors which probably should be taken into account. First, the film was made for US television exposure but to be shown elsewhere in cinemas, which is what happened to those adaptations of British literary classics by American director Delbert Mann – *David Copperfield* (1970) and *Jane Eyre* (1971), both for Omnibus Productions, which also made his *Kidnapped* (1971). All three of these films had stellar British casts and all more or less sank without trace: they are all respectful, respectable and, apart from the odd enjoyable cameo from some or other gifted British actor, devoid of interest.

Second, the film was originally intended as a musical. Perhaps the film's makers were inspired by the commercial and critical success of Carol Reed's Oscar-winning *Oliver!* (1968), the musical version of *Oliver Twist*, but the very qualified reception given to Ronald Neame's musical *Scrooge* (1971), from *A Christmas Carol*, and the general thumbs-down to Michael Tuchner's murky *Mr Quilp* (1974), from *The Old Curiosity Shop*, ought to have given Hardy's producers pause. As noted above, *Great Expectations* is one of Dickens's most closely wrought and darkly imagined works: it would have required major musical talents not simply to interfere with and dilute the dramatic action. There was some publicity in 1974 to the film's ditching of its musical aspirations. *CinemaTV Today* reported that 'In an unprecedented move, the bulk of the score for Sir Lew Grade and NBC's (NBC is the American distributor) musical version of "Great Expectations" has been scrapped seven weeks into shooting'.[1]

Films Illustrated, two months later, reported: 'Originally the film was to have been a musical but ... the decision has been reversed and it will now contain only a traditional score by Maurice Jarre'.[2] And in 1995 Michael York recalled:

> This started out as a musical. But what we found when we started putting it together was the songs interrupted the narrative flow of the piece. I was singing things like 'I have great expectations', all very nice, but Dickens is too entertaining in himself.[3]

Or as York wrote elsewhere, 'Instead of counterpointing, illuminating or ideally advancing the action, it was found that they stopped it dead.'[4]

It is only worth labouring this point because there is, in fact, a feeling of such attenuation about the film that it keeps suggesting something is missing, a suspicion that we have been left with a curiously drained film. In a word, then, neither of these intertextual elements – the pallid 'literary classics' for television nor the musicalisation of Dickens – was likely to augur well for Hardy's film. And in the event, it is pretty much as unsatisfactory as *The Listener*'s reviewer claimed when he wrote: 'Everything is wrong about it with a sort of dedicated, inspired wrongness that, in itself, is breath-

[1] Anon, 'What the Dickens?', *CinemaTV Today*, 17 August 1974, p. 1.

[2] Anon, 'The musical that never was', *Films Illustrated*, October 1974, p. 53.

[3] 'Michael York' in Brian McFarlane (ed), *An Autobiography of British Cinema*. London: Methuen/British Film Institute, 1997, p. 619.

[4] Michael York, *Accidentally on Purpose: An Autobiography*. New York: Simon & Schuster, 1991, p. 290.

taking'.[5] Hardy is on record as saying: 'I hope people won't feel the necessity of comparing it with David Lean's film because it's quite different.'[6] He need not have worried: no one would have spoken of them in the same breath. It's not just Lean's film with which it would not stand comparison but with several superior TV mini-series too. We accept that, in adapting a long novel to the demands of a two-hour film, some ellipsis will be necessary, but the over-all effect is of something that has been sanitised for musical treatment, then demusicalised, so that there is no roughness, pain or harshness remaining, only an insipid, sentimental simplification of its great antecedent. Interestingly, there were later reports 'that a version *with the songs* (italics in original) was to be staged in either Great Britain or Canada with the inspired casting of John Mills and Jean Simmons – this time in the roles of Magwitch and the older Estella. Nothing yet has come of the plan.'[7]

It is as though this film has recognised the significance of the three stages in Dickens's novel and accordingly divides itself into three sections with titles announcing: THE BEGINNING 1830, LONDON 1836, and THE RETURN 1850, but apart from its tripartite nature there is not much sense of parallel. Here, the earliest section lasts 55 minutes, the London section 35 minutes, and the final section 34, and this latter is devoid of the moral dimension with which Dickens (and, briefly, Lean) imbues it. In fairness it should be added that most versions devote more time to the events of Dickens's first 'stage' in Pip's career and it is interesting to wonder why this should be so. It is clearly important to ensure our sympathetic involvement with Pip and to make us fully aware of

[5] Gavin Millar, ' Cinema: Gags and knickers', *The Listener*, 22 January 1976, p. 88.
[6] Anon, 'The musical that never was', op cit.
[7] Alvin H. Marill, 'The Television Scene', *Films in Review*, March 1982, p. 188.

what will prove the formative influences of his life: the terrifying encounter with Magwitch, the meeting with Miss Havisham and Estella, and, though he will not be aware of its significance until he is very much older, the simple human kindness of Joe.

Hardy opens the film in near-monochrome as Pip (Simon Gipps-Kent) lingers in the foggy churchyard by his parents' grave, while the voice of the grown Pip (York) is heard on the soundtrack. This verbal echo of the novel, 'My father's family name being Pirrip ...' etc, is peculiarly tenacious in the many adaptations, perhaps because of its way of ending by focusing our attention on the 'small bundle of shivers growing afraid of it all'; on Pip, that is, just as the wintry bleakness of the setting is invaded by Magwich, an effect unforgettably rendered by Lean in 1946. Hardy, as Gordon Gow noted at the time, 'is at least sensible enough to do otherwise than Lean, whose method of astonishment cannot be topped ... (and) has the convict rising up slowly behind Pip, seen first by the audience but not by the boy.'[8] As colour seeps gradually into Freddie Young's cinematography, we can be pardoned for having our own expectations, but they are soon dashed. The encounter between Pip and the convict is tamely rendered, with James Mason playing intelligently, of course, but in such a subdued way that the child's terror doesn't seem as firmly based as it might be. When they re-meet on the marshes, the all-important look that passes between them, the look on which Pip's fortunes will depend, is so perfunctorily done that it might almost be missed by those not expecting it.

As for the Gargery household, it is somewhat disconcertingly set in the village street, not bleakly on the edge of the marshes, and, like the village street itself, is all too redolent of a Christmas-card

[8] Gordon Gow, *'Great Expectations'*, *Films and Filming*, March 1976, p. 35.

idea of Dickens. Dickens, holding 'no brief for village life',[9] in Mrs Leavis's previously quoted phrase, would scarcely have cared for this prettified account. The house is a comparatively cosy affair, with willow-pattern dinner service on the dresser, Windsor chairs and other such appurtenances that any self-respecting antiques dealer would snap up. In this comfortable-looking ambience, Rachel Roberts' genuinely alarming Mrs Joe strikes a surprisingly vicious note, but again, as in the opening moments, the film sticks very closely to the language of the original, as it does in the Christmas Day dinner. Here the guests are reduced to Uncle Pumblechook and Mr and Mrs Hubble (omitting the thematically more important Wopsle, another villager who, in Dickens, tries his arm in the big city). As always in the filmed versions, Pip, fleeing the table before his culinary thefts on Magwich's behalf are discovered, runs against the sergeant's legs, as if no film-maker could resist the visual invitation offered by the novel at this point. All of this is skimpily treated, though that need not matter; nor need the conflation of this visit with Pumblechook's much later (in the novel) bringing of the news that Miss Havisham wants a boy to come to Satis House to 'play'.

The cardinal functions (as outlined in detail at the beginning of this book) – Pip does Magwich's bidding; Pip goes to Satis House, and so on – are preserved; that is, those narrative hinge-points or risky moments, in Barthes' phrase,[10] capable of more than one outcome, still propel the plot, but they are largely divested of those 'integrational functions' or 'indices' which denote a 'more or less

[9] Q.D. Leavis, 'How we must read *Great Expectations*', in F.R. Leavis and Q.D. Leavis, *Dickens the Novelist*. Harmondsworth: Penguin, 1972, p. 392.

[10] Roland Barthes, 'Introduction to the Structural Analysis of Narratives' (1966), in *Image-Music-Text*, trans. Stephen Heath. Glasgow: Fontana/Collins, 1977, p. 93.

diffuse concept which is nevertheless necessary to the meaning of the story'.[11] By this I mean the ways in which, for example, notations of character such as Magwich's perception of what Pip has done for him, or the idea of Joe as repository of the virtues on which Pip will turn his back, or the kinds of narrow pomposity and folly represented by the dinner guests, help to form our understanding of the world which Pip will leave. Merely to retain the skeleton of events from the antecedent text is no guarantee of retaining its affective or intellectual impact – if that was the film-maker's aim. When Mrs Joe is found collapsed on her kitchen floor, the cardinal function is retained but it is so abruptly presented, with no concern for its cause, that it passes for almost nothing. It is the means of inserting Biddy into the household, but since the film deletes Orlick, who, as we have seen earlier, has an important symbolic function in the novel, the incident totally lacks resonance. It is not, for instance, explored in terms of 'transferred guilt' as it is in the novel.

The film fares slightly better in its representation of Satis House and its inhabitants. The journey there, which Pip undertakes with Pumblechook, is through what seems like a prosperous market town and the first view of Satis House suggests a handsome property somewhat fallen into neglect. According to the information available, this town and its street and Satis House itself seem likely to have been recreated on the Shepperton back-lot,[12] and it is adequately done without there being any sign of character or imagination about it. Inside, the film's colour adds nothing to the ghostly chiaroscuro of Lean's film, but the first glimpse of Miss Havisham is genuinely strange, drawing closely on the visual cues of Dickens's account of how Pip first sees her: 'I saw that everything

[11] Ibid, p. 92.
[12] 'The musical that never was', op cit.

within my view which ought to be white, had been white long ago, and had lost its lustre, and was faded and yellow (Ch. VIII).' In Margaret Leighton's interpretation of the jilted recluse, there is less hint of the imperious madness that made Martita Hunt's interpretation seem definitive, but there is instead a potent sense of the perverse pleasure she takes in watching Estella humiliate Pip, and, during a later visit, of real cruelty in her telling him, 'You've lost her'. But if Leighton injects a necessary bitterness into these scenes, the production design is too tasteful, not gothic enough, to 'belong' to its semi-demented owner. As for Estella, there is some sense of rightness in her being played throughout by Sarah Miles: the Estella of this film, as in Dickens's novel, is in so many ways 'older' than Pip that the film makes a point by having this difference established during their childhood scenes. That is, Estella has already reached, been moulded into, a sort of maturity, while Pip is at this stage very much a naïve boy. Gordon Gow, however, thought it odd to have 'Pip thus divided between two players, (while) his beloved Estella should be played by one actress the whole way through'.[13]

So, the film takes nearly half its running time for the business of Pip's childhood and his growing into the blacksmith's apprentice (Gipps-Kent grows convincingly enough into York). His vulnerability is established, though the young actor is somewhat stiff and inexpressive. The village and the forge are cosily at odds with the grim march of events, though not to any dramatic contrastive effect. The main influences on Pip's subsequent life – Magwich, Miss Havisham, Estella, Joe and Jaggers – are adequately sketched, Quayle's Jaggers having been several times singled out for critical

[13] Gow, p. 36.

praise. The *Monthly Film Bulletin*, indeed, finished its review with: `...
and only Anthony Quayle as Jaggers manages to preserve some of
the grim sidelong humour of the original.'[14] He is at least allowed to
retain Dickens's great line about Jaggers' `large experience of
boys' whom he knows to be `a bad set of fellows' (Ch. VIII).

The central London section records Pip's relationship with
Herbert Pocket (played with engaging cheeriness by former child
star, Andrew Ray), with Bentley Drummle (James Faulkner), who, for
reasons of easily introducing him into the plot, has rooms below Pip
and Herbert's, and with Jaggers. Jaggers' pervasive sense of
knowing all that needs to be known of London crime and its
prosecution is much reduced and the single hand-washing, so
potently suggestive a *habit* in the novel, is no more than a brief
catalytic function here (i.e., small action with no thematic or
narrative resonance[15]), and Wemmick, again of more indicial
importance than crucial to cardinal functions in Dickens, is reduced
to the barest pop-eyed appearance by Peter Bull. The film's elliptic
practices are very apparent here: for instance, the business of Pip's
asking Jaggers to find lucrative employment for Herbert comes so
quickly as to seem unmotivated by events; and Joe's visit to
London, so important in the growth of Pip's self-knowledge in the
novel, is reduced to no more than its news-bearing function, a
typical `reduction' of this superficial film. Pip denies Joe to
Drummle, describing Joe as `my blacksmith', this unsubtle explicit-
ness eliding any sense of Pip's growing shame and irritation with
Joe. As for Pip's London `education' or for how he falls into
spendthrift, snobbish ways, these pass for almost nothing. The
montage of social occasions – ballroom, gallery, riding, archery,

[14] Sylvia Millar, *Monthly Film Bulletin*, December 1975, p. 261.
[15] Barthes, op cit, pp. 93–94.

and longer ballroom sequence – echoes a similar pattern in Lean's film and to the same purpose: Pip's increasing infatuation with Estella and the growth of his jealousy of the boorish Drummle.

This whole London section leads, as in the novel, to the return of Magwich (a symbolic return of what Pip has repressed of his origins) on a wild night. Since the preceding events have been too rushed for motivation and relationship to emerge in detail and clarity, since there has been so little sense of Pip's having become an idler and a snob, the climactic return of the convict whose fortune has endowed Pip goes for less than it might. Mason's Magwich is at pains not to replicate the alarming, farouche effect of Finlay Currie's in the earlier film, and it is seriously acted in an understated way, but it simply doesn't seem unnerving enough to account for its supposed effect on Pip. In fact he suggests a more or less benevolent country uncle rather than a terrifying revenant. But then, this whole London section suffers from an almost total failure to make the city itself palpable or menacing. The production design skimps on the representation of its streets, so that one has no sense of what Pip is responding to: it is as though there is no more to this film's idea of London than what is glimpsed in the montage of its fashionable life.

In the film's final section, 'The Return', there is a brief shot of a London street in which the scarred convict (not named as Compeyson and having nothing to do with Miss Havisham, thus loosening the narrative web of the original) follows Herbert as he leaves the steamship office where he has been making arrangements for Magwich's escape. But this shot is too fleeting to make any impression relating to the possible dangers of the city, and the subsequent sequence set on the foggy river by night, the setting for the foiling of the escape plans, is utterly perfunctory. Lean's decision to film this by day rather than swathed in night mist seems

more than ever to have been the right one. In Hardy's hands, the
episode is devoid of excitement, and the ensuing sequence in
which Pip visits the dying Magwich in the prison hospital is similarly
skimped. James Mason may be on record as saying: 'one of my
favourite roles, in any medium, is the convict Magwitch (*sic*) in
Great Expectations,[16] but it is hard to see on what grounds, in the
light of what he is given to do in this film. The point of drawing
attention to the way these episodes are simply rushed past, as if
their task was just to give narrative information of the most basic
kind, is to underline the film's failure to make anything of Pip's moral
reclamation, a matter so powerfully present in the novel.

The other key aspect of this final section, Pip's re-meeting with
Estella, is not so much rushed as sentimentalised. When Pip returns
to the village after eleven years abroad, it is Christmas Eve again,
the streets as picturesquely as before evoking 'Quality Street' toffee
tins, and Pumblechook (some distance from Dickens's pompous
hypocrite) is comfortably ensconced in the Gargery kitchen. Joe
has married Biddy in the film's first section and they now have a
young son called Pip. The older Pip leaves this cosy domestic scene
to visit the now ruined Satis House which is about to be pulled
down. As Pip walks through the snowy desolation of its grounds and
dilapidated halls, in one of the film's few visually arresting sequences,
he imagines he hears Estella's voice from the past, prior to finding
her sitting, veiled, in Miss Havisham's old chair, as in Lean's film. Just
for a moment the film achieves a compelling sense of two people
having been brought back to this place by forces larger than
themselves. 'What ridiculous children we were,' she says, 'both
trying to master our own lives'. Quickly, though, the film gives way
to clichés of sentimentality: Estella improbably tells Pip: 'I loved you

[16] Quoted in Marill, op cit.

from the first moment I saw you', claiming that she has only married Drummle (now dead) to save Pip from ruining his life.

In these last moments, the film is visually superior (it is after all shot by the Oscar-winning cinematgrapher Freddie Young) to its verbal content, and the long, upward back-tracking shot that sees them walking away from Satis House has a certain grace and discretion. By this stage, however, it is hard to care about a film which has flattened out most possibilities for truer, harsher insights. It has retained the novel's cardinal functions to a considerable extent, but has failed to imbue these with the kinds of 'felt life' of Henry James's phrase, and has failed to make them matter in terms of character and relationship, so that they remain largely a recital of events. The writing is surely most seriously at fault: Sherman Yellen's screenplay allows actors almost no scope for doing more than going through their narrative paces. Even so, every now and then a character suggests an inner life (as well as a touch of Dickens, always perhaps an acceptable bonus in a film derived from him) that redeems the general flatness. Quayle's Jaggers has been mentioned earlier and he, wisely making no attempt to emulate Francis L. Sullivan's magisterial incarnation in 1946, has an impressive gravitas. Additionally, David Parker is right, in my view, to single out Joss Ackland's Joe: 'Ackland manages to create a subtle blend of individual simplicity and moral fortitude that seems to capture the essential role the village blacksmith fills in the narrative.'[17] (Sylvia Millar, though, claims that Joe is reduced to 'a cardboard nonentity of rural dignity.'[18]) However, both these admirable actors are working with meagre help from a screenplay which gives them scant running time and little scope to suggest the

[17] David Parker, www.screenonline.org.uk/film/id/473459
[18] Sylvia Millar, op cit.

range of their characters' influence. In the leads, York and, especially Miles, work hard to invest their characters with some sense of emotional development, and are quite touching in their final suggestions of having been wrought and chastised by experience. Miles, nevertheless, was under no illusions about the film, later claiming: 'I knew that the film would never be more than a worthy attempt', nearly turning it down because of 'the slim chance of repeating such classy stuff (as the Lean film)'.[19]

Despite these minor rewards, however, it has to be said that the film really fails on almost every count. The *Monthly Film Bulletin* accuses director Hardy and screenwriter Yellen of 'reduc(ing) one of Dickens' most subtle and complex novels to an insipid seasonal confection',[20] claiming that '... this version denudes an untidy masterpiece of all terror, mystery, irony, humour and psychological depth.' This is a severe judgment, but it is matched by *The Listener*'s reviewer:

> Great swathes have been cast out of the plot, and what remains lacks flavour, suspense, accuracy and, most important of all, the gravity that makes this one of Dickens's most serious treatments of class, crime and moral culpability.[21]

These harsh judgements are worth considering in relation to the film as just another film *and* as an adaptation of Dickens. Taking it simply as a *Bildungsfilm*, the film is so perfunctory about the forces working on Pip – the wish to be a gentleman, how this affects his attitudes to those he has grown up with, how he reacts to wealth, how he

[19] Sarah Miles, *Bolt from the Blue*. London: Phoenix, 1996, p. 32.
[20] Sylvia Millar, op cit.
[21] Gavin Millar, op cit.

responds to the unwelcome revelation of his benefactor's identity and so on – that the relative weights of these influences are scarcely felt. In terms neither psychological (e.g., the importance of 'father figures') nor cinematic (e.g., in matters relating to cinematography or editing) does the film venture beyond the most commonplace narrative recital. What, for instance, does the film want us to make of the sorts of paternal influence we must suppose to be exerted by Joe, Magwich or Jaggers? Compare its vacancy in this matter with Anny Sadrin's thoughtful discussion of the extent to which the first two may or may not be considered as father figures in Pip's life.[22] In Freddie Young's Technicolor photography there is no scope for ambiguity, for suggestive darkness: Young is so gifted a cinematographer that we can only assume his hands were tied in this matter, that he was instructed to keep it all flat and bright, suitable not so much for the big screen as for US television screens. That other distinguished collaborator, costume designer Elizabeth Haffenden, has somewhat more success: the costumes sometimes make their point when the screenplay is inhibiting the actors from doing so. For instance, Pip's striped silk dressing-gown patronises Joe whose visit to London, so crucial in the novel, passes for so little here; and the life-wearied Estella's ponderous gown in the last sequence mutely attests to the intervening years.

For all that one adheres to the notion that a film, adaptation or not, must be primarily judged on how it stands as a film, it is hard to suppress the feeling that if Hardy *et al* had taken serious heed of what Dickens was up to, they might have made a more engrossing film. If, for example, he had thought harder about how Pip's story could be made to critique a society in which the rigidities of class

---

[22] Anny Sadrin, *Parentage and inheritance in the novels of Charles Dickens*. Cambridge: Cambridge University Press, pp. 108–111.

matter so much; or if he had more rigorously pursued the culpability of adults who wrench young lives out of their likely course without adequately considering the possible consequences; or if he had shown more interest in the kinds of love that expand or wound the heart; all these matters are at stake in Dickens's novel, one of the richest and most mature he ever wrote. However much one insists on the autonomy of a film derived from a novel, it is still hard to resist such evaluative comparisons, especially when the original is a kind of masterpiece. Michael York wrote sixteen years after making the film:

> Dickens seemed ideal for television, writing as he did in serial form for the penny press with a superabundance of personages and plots. Indeed, the problem was that his characters were so compelling they were difficult to restrain or ignore. Our two-hour film was obliged to be just as much a condensation and extrapolation as David Lean's celebrated earlier version had been.[23]

True enough, one supposes, but the critical issue has to do with what has been omitted, how the 'condensation' has been managed, to what extent has 'extrapolation' been guided by a wish to retain events or characters or in the interests of some over-arching, controlling principle. Some thematic intention that would give resonance and coherence to the events which make up the plot? It is hard to quarrel with the writer who described it as 'an adequate if uninspired and unnecessary remake'.[24] It is not just that it lacks the psychological and social dimensions that make the

[23] York, op cit, p. 200.

[24] Sheridan Morley, *James Mason: Odd Man Out.* London: Weidenfeld & Nicolson, 1989, p. 161.

original so powerful and disturbing; it also irons out Dickens's relish for the melodramatic, that flair for which helps to account for his being so great an entertainer. We can most **easily** imagine Hardy's film as a Christmas afternoon television **programme** whose sated viewers won't feel they've missed much if they doze off.

great expectations (1998): from estuary to gulf, to manhattan and back

••

Mexican director Alfonso Cuarón's 1998 film is the loosest version yet of *Great Expectations*: loosest, that is, in the sense of taking just what it likes from Dickens and heedlessly jettisoning the rest. It is also at least arguably the most wholly re-imagined, and that includes Lean's. It is generally quite unDickensian in feeling (e.g., it is not setting out to replicate 'atmosphere' or verbal 'tone'), but that is neither here nor there: to be 'Dickensian' (and that can embrace a range of concepts) has always seemed to me to be no more than one of the possibilities open to the film adaptor of his works. The basic story of Dickens's novel is there in outline in Cuarón's film; if this were not so it would hardly qualify as an adaptation and it would seem to play false with audience expectations.

The intertexuality of this latest version most notably includes not only Dickens's novel but also Lean's film, Cuarón's film constituting a 'hypertext' in relation to the two previous 'hypotexts', to employ Genette's useful terminology.

> ... the category that occupies Genette most centrally in *Palimpsestes*, and the one that has the most direct bearing on cinematic remakes, is the fourth type, hypertextuality. Genette

> defines hypertextuality as the relationship between a given text (the 'hypertext') and an anterior text (the hypotext) that it transforms.[1]

The sense of indebtedness in Cuarón's film is perhaps most strongly felt in the film's opening sequence, where it is up against stiff competition from the two anterior texts, but it emerges more than honourably. A boy in a boat in the Florida Gulf country stops the boat, takes out a sketch-book and pencils and walks through the shallow water, as the voice-over, presumably belonging to him, reflects that: 'There either is or is not a way things are. The colour of the day, the way it felt to be a child, the feeling of salt water on your sunburnt legs. Sometimes the water is yellow, sometimes it is red, but what colour it may be in memory depends on the day. I'm not going to tell the story the way it happened; I'm going to tell it the way I remember it.' Birds circle the boy, Finn (Jeremy James Kissner); as he sketches fish and stars, the camera records fish leaping in the transparent water, and executes graceful moves about the boy, creating both sensuous serenity and tension, both shattered by the appearance of the shackled convict Lustig (Robert De Niro) from the shallow water. The *Variety* reviewer at the time noted accurately enough: 'The convict's visually startling but physically implausible rise out of the surf underscores the film's premise that the events on view are presented as Finn remembers them years later, not necessarily the way they happened.'[2]

[1] Andrew Horton and Stuart Y. McDougal (eds). *Play It Again Sam: Retakes on Remakes*. Berkeley: University of California Press, 1998, p. 3 (eScholarship: http://ark.cdlib.org/ark:/13030/ft1j49n6d3/).

[2] Todd McCarthy, *Great Expectations*, *Variety*, January 19–25, 1998, p. 88.

Both Dickens and Lean, without announcing it so explicitly, make clear that the ensuing narrative will be the result of memory: Dickens is writing in the past tense which implies recollection by a memory much older than the observing small child; Lean accompanies the image of the novel's opening page with the grown Pip's voice on the soundtrack reading the first sentences. We know in both that we are in the hands of a narrator whose memories we shall have to trust: Cuarón just spells this out. His relation to the hypotexts continues with the eruption of the convict who leaps at the boy, towering over him and threatening him in a modern vernacular that, if he tells anyone about this encounter, 'I'll pull out yer fuckin' insides and make you eat them ... I'll fuckin' kill you if you betray me'. The sense of shock and of the child's terror is as potent here as in either of the great precursors, the violent incursion of the convict into the child's life and the voice-over insistently reminding us of the latter. Memory and voice-over: these are two crucial elements in this latest version.

In an interview Gwyneth Paltrow, the grown-up Estella, quite astutely assessed the film's relationship to the novel: 'Listen, we're taking certain dynamics between the characters, we're taking certain structural arcs, and that's it. Then we're colouring it in a completely different way ...'[3] In general terms, that's a fair comment. This is a pared-down version of the novel (as of course they all are), but the central characters and the trajectories of their lives still exhibit the lineaments Dickens created for them, but the 'colouring', to use Paltrow's term, belongs distinctively to Cuarón, his screenwriter Mitch Glazer, and his brilliant cinematographer Emmanuel Lubezki, with whom he had worked several times before. Let's consider the two main elements in the Paltrow comment.

[3] Quoted in P.J. Sloane, 'The sweetest perfection', in *Film Review*, May 1998, p. 49.

Structural arcs

Like all the film versions of *Great Expectations*, this 1998 adaptation fails to maintain the almost exactly equal space which Dickens allows to the three 'stages' of Pip's career (it is interesting to speculate on why he is here called Finn: a name that 'connects him with another nineteenth-century orphan, Mark Twain's Huck Finn',[4] or at a lower punning level with the fish he draws as they leap through the water). Like the earlier films it offers a full account of the childhood and youth up to the point of his leaving the village (44 of the present film's 111 minutes) and roughly the same for chronicling his rise in the big city, then a rush to bring matters to a conclusion, as if the kind of moral resurgence in the disillusioned protagonist, which is so important in Dickens, might be less engrossing when depicted cinematically.

In regard to Pip/Finn, the structural arc more or less holds. He is thrust out of security by the convict Lustig, who enjoins on him a fearful secrecy and the need to steal from his sister Maggie (food from the refrigerator) and 'Uncle' Joe (bolt-cutters). This upheaval in Finn's life is then paralleled by another that will prove to have far-reaching effects: he is summoned by the local recluse, Nora Dinsmoor (Anne Bancroft), standing in for Miss Havisham, with whose niece Estella (as a child, Raquel Baudene) he is com-manded to play. When Estella is sent abroad, Finn tries to settle to the mundane life of a fisherman with Joe (Chris Cooper), when another disruption occurs: a lawyer, Jerry Ragno (Josh Mostel), acting as Jaggers does elsewhere, arrives. 'I'm empowered by my client to make your dreams come true,' he advises. This time, what is being offered is the chance to live and work in New York as an

[4] Michael K. Johnson, 'Not Telling the Story the Way It Happened: Alfonso Cuarón's *Great Expectations*', *Film/Literature Quarterly*, Vol. 33, No.1, 2005, p. 67.

artist; Finn, who has given up painting, grabs the chance, finds success, loses his moral bearings but re-finds Estella; is confronted with the source of his income when Lustig re-enters his life; holds Lustig when he is shot by a former associate; and returns to the Gulf to find Joe, happily married and with a child, and an experience-matured Estella.

To turn to Estella, the discernible arc is there. She has been trained to hurt men by her deranged aunt, Nora, who tells Finn: 'She'll only break your heart ... You already love her ... even though I warn you she'll only hurt you terribly.' The haughty young girl, who carelessly tosses aside Finn's drawing of her, is sent to France for seven years and re-surfaces in New York, where she uses Finn as bait to spur on a slow-moving suitor. She allows Finn one act of sexual consummation before disappearing from his life until the final segment when he and the divorced Estella are reunited outside the ruins of Nora Dinsmoor's mansion. Their hands touch in a final moment which approximates to the subdued promise of Dickens's revised last paragraph.

In terms of the 54 major cardinal functions I have identified (see chapter one), it is arguable that Glazer and Cuarón have retained no more than 19, and that figure is only reached if such analogies as 'Lustig dies in the subway train' for 'Magwitch dies in prison' are accepted.[5] I think they *are* acceptable since the 'hinge-point'[6] effect of the function is retained, even though the informants (including names and place names, e.g., Finn for Pip; 'Paradiso Perdito' for 'Satis House') have been changed and some of the

[5] The cardinal functions retained in recognisable form are 1–4, 8, 10, 15–16, 19, 21–23, 33–34, 39, 47, 50, 53–54 (see my list on pp. 9–11.

[6] Roland Barthes, 'Introduction to the Structural Analysis of Narratives' (1966), in *Image-Music-Text*, trans. Stephen Heath. Glasgow: Fontana/Collins, 1977, p. 93.

indices, which relate to concepts of character and atmosphere have been clearly altered. For instance, Finn's sister, now called Maggie, is sluttish rather than shrewish and the atmosphere of the house in which she and Finn live with 'Uncle' Joe is not the Spartan establishment presided over by Mrs Joe in the novel. In the words of Finn's voice-over, 'I was raised in what I suppose was a certain amount of freedom by my sister Maggie. Joe was her man'. This kind of supportive detail has no effect on the 'structural arc' of which Paltrow speaks, any more than Propp's account of narrative functions of characters is influenced by their 'distinctive, vivid colouring':[7] that is, by such matters as personality traits or motivation. Important as these are to our reception of a narrative, they are not to be confused with its underlying structure. I shall return to the notion of 'colouring' shortly.

Dynamics between characters

Great Expectations (1998) retains at its centre the way in which its two central characters – Finn and Estella – are each manipulated by another who has an agenda to pursue. Estella has been trained by her aunt Nora Dinsmoor who 'lost her mind thirty years ago when her fiancé left her standing at the altar' as the voice-over informs us. In the garden of her Mediterranean-style mansion, 'Paradiso Perdito', with its echoes of Venice and of the Alhambra, are candelabra and urns, no doubt wedding gifts, long since over-grown and covered in weeds, but, alongside the evidence of decay, with a curious luxuriance of growth. Joe has made a business call on Miss Dinsmoor and Estella has sighted Pip; this leads to a telephone call to Maggie, who shrilly urges Joe to take

[7] V. Propp, *Morphology of the Folktale* (1927), trans. Laurence Scott. Austin: University of Texas, 1968, p. 75.

advantage of this, just as Finn is watching on television the arrest of 'his' convict. Lustig, the reporter says, is 'scheduled to die on March 16 by lethal injection'. In this neat manner, the two agents of manipulation are juxtaposed: just as Finn is to be brought into the orbit of Estella's aunt, who has already wrenched her niece's life out of its normal course, the man who will prove to be Finn's benefactor is making the news – while Finn will come to believe that Nora is also his benefactress, planning him for Estella.

The most crucial 'dynamics' between characters are of course those between Finn and Estella and in this respect Cuarón and Glazer have retained the contours laid down by Dickens but updated them convincingly to the end of the twentieth century. Finn is humiliated by Estella when he makes his first invited appearance at 'Paradiso Perdito' and the following exchange between him and Nora echoes the same situation in the novel:

'What do you think of her?'
'I think she's a snob.'
'Anything else?'
'I think she's real pretty.'
'Anything else?'
'I think she doesn't like me.'
'But you love her. She'll only break your heart ...'

And then, 'I'd like to go now.'

This is accompanied by a rapid exchange of looks between Finn and Estella, or rather of Finn *at* Estella who is revealed in a montage of the facial parts of this exquisite girl, who on showing Pip out encourages him to drink with her at an outdoor fountain. She then kisses him most sensuously, as if she already knows her power over him.

In a dissolve that elides the visits Finn pays to Paradiso Perdito, the children turn into their adult counterparts played by Ethan Hawke and Paltrow. 'The money Dinsmoor paid me kept me in paints and brushes (cf. Miss Havisham's paying for Pip's indentures in the novel) ... and there *was* Estella', the unusually insistent first-person voice-over tells us. Estella, being launched socially by Nora, is going to 'that cocktail thing' to which Finn offers to escort her, but the security guard refuses him admittance in Joe's scruffy pick-up truck as other guests enter with effortless ease. Estella appears and asks him provocatively 'Do you want to get me out of here?' and asks him to take her to 'Your house'. Once there, he experiences some sense of shame at the clutter, mocking in self-deprecation what she'd first told him about the European affiliations of Nora's architecture. She prowls his and Joe's house (Maggie has gone), and sets about seducing him, her bare thigh pressing against his hands, and she swoons as his hand seeks out her crotch. This is extremely sexy stuff, overtly replacing Pip's romantic obsession with something much more sensual on Finn's part, but, as in Dickens, it is she who makes the running. She gets him very excited, then walks away, leaving with a cool remark in French about how she is going abroad tomorrow.

That there should be no misunderstanding of the manipulation involved here, the film then turns to Finn's running to Paradiso Perdito, where Nora, 'weirder than usual', tells him how 'twenty-six years ago she was a virgin: 'What kind of creature takes advantage of a forty-two-year-old? A man does this ... So men must pay. Estella will make men weep ... She'll break them. I taught her well. She'll cut through them like a hot knife through butter.' Throughout this and other episodes, Bancroft's Nora is dressed in a series of outré, greenish garments, their sub-aqueous colouring allying her with the water from which that other manipulator, Lustig, has leapt into Finn's life. Both these manipulators must die for the book's structure to reach its closure, and so it is in this film version: the modes of their deaths are strikingly different from those in the novel, but their importance in the dynamics between characters is more or less the same. Lustig's danger and murder inspire some responsive feeling from Finn; Estella has broken free from her aunt but she has married unsuccessfully, despite her greater freedom of action.

In lesser but still important ways, the dynamics are retained, despite shifts in time and place and all the changes of *mores* these shifts necessarily bring in their wake. For instance, Joe remains the key influence on Finn's boyhood: it is he who gives Finn the advice 'Just be yourself' when Finn is dressing to take Estella to the fashionable party from which he is excluded. Later, when Joe comes to New York he exposes the snobbish falsity that Finn has fallen prey to: Joe knocks over a tray-load of champagne glasses and stoops to pick up the pieces to Finn's embarrassed irritation, just as Pip had seethed at Joe Gargary's exploits with a coffee cup in London. In this sense, Joe is a catalyst for the clear revealing of how Finn has changed. Other examples of how character dynamics have been retained include the use of the lawyer Ragno to act as intermediary between his anonymous client and legatee Finn, though Ragno's personality is more benign than that of Dickens's Jaggers. The engagement of Estella to the socially suitable but unendearing Walter, who wonders if Finn is Estella's 'charming little version of a wake-up call' to nudge him into commitment, recalls how Dickens's Estella used the egregious Bentley Drummle to fire Pip's jealousy – and possibly Pip's presence to irk Drummle. In these ways, major and lesser, the pattern of relationships created in the Dickensian hypotext are reproduced in their essence here.

Distinctive colouring

Linking Propp and Paltrow is perhaps not the first connection that comes to mind, but both use the word 'colouring' to account for matters extraneous to the deeper structures at work in narratives of whatever degree of sophistication. This is not to relegate those other elements of the novel or the film to subsidiary places but merely to distinguish between two different orders of narrative 'activity' in each. As well as telling a story and creating complex interactions of characters, Dickens's novel also offers a stinging social critique of a class-bound society. It is clear that he intends the reader to respond to the way true gentility, in its now-outmoded sense of characterising the true gentleman, has no reliable connection with wealth or social position. From this point of view, clumsy, loving Joe, endowed with the defining characteristics of placing concern for others above his own needs, of generosity and forgivingness and other such qualities, and the gentle, decent, none-too-competent Herbert Pocket (for whom there is no character equivalent in this film) are the positives against which the cruelties of class may be measured. A figure like Magwitch can be seen as the victim of a system that seems designed to keep such as he in subjection.

What does Cuarón's film offer in this respect? The answer is not very much. There is some social sense at work in Finn's early humiliations at Estella's hands and at being discriminated against by the security guard at the society party. One assumes that Cuarón and Glazer intend the superficialities of the New York art world to stand in for Dickens's more comprehensive and far-reaching critique, but it is too comparatively insignificant to bear much weight, and the arty types are too conventionally sketched. Finn's big show is meant to 'represent the fulfillment (sic) of both his expectations – to have the girl, to be an artistic success. Estella's absence reveals the failure of his romantic quest, and the convict's return undermines his vision of himself as an artistic success.'[8] It works, that is, in narrative terms, but only in a vestigial way as social criticism.

However, the film's 'distinctive colouring' does not lie in this direction so much as in the overtly sexual character with which it imbues Finn's quest. It is easy to see why, if the idea of updating and transplanting Dickens's novel is to work, the film-makers would feel the need to dispose of the concept of 'the making of a gentleman'. Such a notion would have been more or less ludicrous in late twentieth-century America. As David Lusted remarks succinctly, 'In the American version (Cuarón's), social class difference is no bar to romance.'[9] Instead of turning Pip into a 'gentleman', Glazer's screenplay gives him the expectation of artistic success. This is one of the ways, and an important one, in which the 1998 film responds to the times in which it is set. Similarly, Estella pursues an unlikely suitor in Walter but does so within the parameters of a freedom not open to Dickens's heroine. As part of the cultural mutations that this new setting makes available to the young protagonists is an attitude to sexual matters that Dickens's characters could not have dreamed of. Well, they may have dreamed of them, as Lean's Pip tells us in voice-over that he does, or as Dickens's Pip imagines he sees 'Estella's face in the fire, with her pretty hair fluttering in the wind and her eyes scorning me' (Ch. XIV), but anything more overtly sensual was out of the question.

Not so here. From the moment the pre-pubescent Estella puts her tongue in Finn's mouth as they are drinking from the same

[8] Johnson, p. 74.

[9] David Lusted, 'Literary adaptations and cultural fantasies', *Journal of Popular British Film*, 4: 2001, p. 78.

fountain in the garden of Paradiso Perdito, this film makes clear that romantic obsession will have an explicitly sexual 'colouring'. (In a comparatively minor matter, too, Finn's sister seems to have been entertaining a lover, or perhaps a sex customer, while Joe is out fishing; and she simply leaves Joe and Finn, rather than dying, and Finn later refers to her as a 'bitch', for which Joe cuffs him.) Years later when Finn and Estella re-meet in New York it is by a fountain in Central Park where she repeats the ardent kiss. Between these two occasions, when they are both grown up, is the provocative episode, referred to above, in which she seems to be leading him on to full consummation in Joe's empty house.

But the key sequence in regard to Finn's obsession with Estella and her knowing collusion with his obsession is the one that takes place in his New York apartment, when he wakes to find her in his bedroom. She strips to skimpy, frilly black underwear, then to nothing, with her back turned to him as he grasps frantically for canvas and sketches her, smudging in her nipples with red and her pubic hair in black. There is a frenzy of music on the soundtrack ('Like a friend,' performed by Pulp) that enacts both her sensual allurement and his sexual and artistic excitement (the latter restraining the former?), and at the end of the modelling session, she announces: 'I have to go. I have dinner in one hour.' She has deliberately lead him on, brought him to a pitch of excitement, then left him, as if to show her power over him, recalling the earlier incident at Joe's house. The *Sight and Sound* reviewer was right to say: 'The high point of the film is a tantalising scene – breathtakingly edited to the music of Pulp – where Estella toys with Finn ...'[10] It is a startlingly sexy scene, much more so than the scene of their ultimate consummation when he has led her away from a fashionable

10 John Wrathall, *'Great Expectations'*, Sight and Sound, May 1998, p. 45.

restaurant and back to his apartment. At the end of this scene, she walks nude to the window in the morning, and next we know of her she is to be married, Nora having come to New York for the wedding. In spite of all the overtly sexual connotations of their scenes together, for the final reunion by the ruins of Paradiso Perdito Cuarón has opted for a return to more romantic mode, and very affecting it is. The sunset stretches beckoningly between them over the Gulf as they stand at the water's edge and they reach for each other's hands. John Wrathall may be right in claiming that the film suffers from 'a lack of emotional weight'[11] but the beautifully lit romanticism of this last moment compensates for a certain loss in Pip/Finn's obsessive quest, especially in Hawke's attractive but too often bland performance. The *Variety* reviewer may well be right when he claims that, despite the persistence of the voice-over, 'Finn doesn't come across as all that interesting, and Hawke provides him with little perceptible inner life or ambition.'[12]

There are other kinds of colouring which give the film its distinctiveness. Anne Bancroft as Nora, the Miss Havisham counterpart, exercises a star charisma to sometimes dazzling effect and the performance suggests that her being jilted when she was on the brink of middle age has indeed deranged her. There is not the implacable bitterness that Martita Hunt brought to the Lean version, but there is a wild, unpredictable sense of a woman who no longer seems to care for anything except her clothes and her old gramophone records – apart, that is, from the grooming of her niece to effect her revenge on men. It is an extravagant but rewarding piece of work, deserving more serious appraisal than one reviewer gave it: 'Bancroft's performance is so over the top

[11] Ibid.
[12] McCarthy, p. 92.

it's amusing. She dances around a decaying Florida mansion as if she's on something.'[13] In an otherwise positive review, John Wrathall considered that Bancroft and De Niro 'play to the gallery shamelessly' and that the return of De Niro's Lustig 'prompts a lurch into melodrama that's unconvincing after the sophistication of what's gone before'.[14] My concern with the presentation of the Magwitch/Lustig character is not so much with De Niro's performance, which it could be argued has an aptly full-blooded quality to it, as with the screenplay's failure to give this character enough sense of past. How did he make his money? Who are these people out to get him? The answers to these questions are perfunctorily implied but without enough detail to make one feel the grateful effort he claims to have made on Finn's behalf. Further, as noted earlier there is very little scope for Finn's redemption as the descent into the subway (metaphorically apt: as Johnson has noted, this coincides with the moment when 'Estella, the star, is elevated into the heavens'[15] on her way out of Finn's life) leads rapidly to Lustig's death.

There are, of course, important colourings other than those relating to character. There is a striking visual responsiveness to the contrast of the serene-looking, easy-going life of the Gulf, epitomised in the casual household in which Joe and Maggie have raised Finn, with both the shabby grandeur of Nora's Moorish-cum-Venetian mansion and the night streets of New York. We might note in passing that what Cuarón can achieve in creating a Dickensian sense of a scruffy, crowded city is better reflected in his *Children of*

[13] Ruthe Stein, 'Modern 'Expectations' Anything But Great', *San Francisco Chronicle*, 30 January 1998.

[14] Wrathall, p. 45.

[15] Johnson, p. 75.

Men, his 2006 film which begins in a London that seems on the brink of collapse. Florida's coast stands in for, without replicating, the atmosphere of Dickens's 'marsh country, down by the river, within as the river wound, twenty miles to the sea'. Pip grows up in a physically much rawer, bleaker landscape and household than Finn does, and this is an example of the way the film intelligently relocates him in time and place while at the same time retaining the bare bones of Dickens's enduring narrative. Lubezki's camera contrives to give the shifting scenes an aura at once realistic and unreal, as if to remind us of Finn's early warning that he is 'going to tell it the way I remember it'. In collusion with Steven Weisberg's editing, the cinematography creates a slumberous sensuousness in the way it, for instance, plays over the young Estella's face; this is as much how Finn remembers it as registering any 'realistic' way of looking at someone. The tilting camera and breathlessly held shots as Estella presents herself to Finn, both in Joe's house and later in New York when she models for him, attest to a cinematic flair that makes something new from the skeleton of a well-known and well-loved story.

Cuarón's *Great Expectations* pays its dues to Dickens and some homage to Lean, but it stands firmly enough on its own to interest those with no knowledge of either of these precursors. It is infinitely to be preferred to either the 1934 Hollywood or 1975 British screen versions which, like it, preserve the outline from Dickens but fill in that outline with nothing of consequence. It is indeed 'a most cinematic venture'[16] as one contemporary reviewer claimed. The director of such diversely accomplished films as a version of Frances Hodgson Burnett's fairy-tale-like *A Little Princess* (1995), employing the same cinematographer, editor and music director (Patrick

[16] James Cameron-Wilson, *'Great Expectations'*, in *Film Review*, May 1998, p. 15.

Doyle) as in his 1998 film, and the Mexican sex-and-road movie, *Y tu mamá también* (2002), and *Children of Men* can here be seen drawing on both the primary strands exhibited in those films. (He shows another sort of interest in youthful aspiration in the darkest of the Rowling adaptations, *Harry Potter and the Prisoner of Azkaban*, 2004.) His *Great Expectations* has a fairy-tale element, as has Dickens's sombre, complex novel; it also offers a genuinely sexy take on that tale of romantic obsession and lives being wrenched out of predictable courses.

great expectations (1946): something like a classic

David Lean's 1946 film has for so long enjoyed the status of an impeccably classic film and classic adaptation that I have deliberately left it until the end of this book to see whether any of the other versions, on screens large or small, might offer a serious challenge to its pre-eminence. They don't. There are, as preceding chapters have aimed at suggesting, real felicities in some of them: in, for example, the 1998 American film and the 1999 British television mini-series, but, in the end, it has to be conceded that none is either as 'Dickensian' or – and this is more important – as distinguished a piece of film-making. This doesn't mean that it is necessarily a flawless film; only that it has approached its project with style and daring and imagination

Contexts
Wartime change
It is worth devoting some space to placing Lean's film in context. (It is *always* worth considering films in their production contexts.) The postwar period may now seem remote to younger readers and filmgoers, but it remains a crucial highpoint in the history of British cinema. The war changed everything about British cinema, as

indeed it did about so much of the national life at large. The cinema of the 1930s has in recent years come in for serious reappraisal[1] but, though it certainly has interests of its own, it now seems indisputably more remote than the films that emerged during and just after the war. The documentary influence, for instance, scarcely impinged on the commercial cinema pre-war. The bulk of 1930s commercial cinema, apart from obvious exceptions such as the films of Alfred Hitchcock, Alexander Korda, Victor Saville and a few others, were modest crime dramas and comedies, with the odd popular musical. The uniformly bad press given to the 'quota quickies' of the period has recently been subject to some scrutiny,[2] suggesting that there may have been more signs of quality than has been allowed, and undeniably some major talents were being nurtured in the period. One of these was David Lean who edited about twenty films during the decade, but who did not direct until 1942.

During the war, British cinema changed dramatically. The influential newspaper critic Dilys Powell wrote: 'It took the war to compel the British to look at themselves and find themselves interesting'.[3] Or as critic Geoff Brown put it: 'For the first time British film-makers had a subject – the war front, the various campaigns – a subject which the Americans couldn't handle. For the first time they had a subject which had a sort of national feeling built into it.'[4] These statements are no doubt true, but to the idea of a

[1] See, for instance, Jeffrey Richards (ed.) *The Unknown 1930s: An Alternative History of the British Cinema, 1929–1939*. London: I.B. Tauris, 1998.

[2] Steve Chibnall, *Quota Quickies: The Birth of the British 'B' Film*. London: BFI Publishing, 2006.

[3] Dilys Powell, 'Films Since 1939', in *Since 1939*. London: Readers' Union and British Council, 1948, p. 83.

[4] Interview with Geoff Brown, London, September, 1989.

'subject' must be added the way in which this subject was handled. A key element of this treatment of both home-front and combat life in the British wartime cinema was some infiltration of documentary approaches in the fiction film, in a way that virtually never occurred in pre-war British cinema. During the war, the fiction film engaged in more detailed observation of real life at work and leisure, so that popular cinema began to reflect more of the experience of everyday life and 'ordinary' people. The critically privileged position of 'realism' in discourse about British cinema for several decades really derives from this period, from films like *Millions Like Us* (1943) and *The Way Ahead* (1944). There were of course other things going on in British wartime cinema, but this particular emphasis is worth noting since it casts a long shadow over subsequent British film.

The literary strand

The other key element in the most critically prized British films of the latter half of the 1940s was the frequency of the literary adaptation. All the most important film-makers of this period — Carol Reed, Michael Powell, Laurence Olivier, the Boulting brothers, Anthony Asquith and Lean – had major successes with films derived from esteemed novels and plays. The mere fact of a film's being adapted from literature does not mean that it is 'literary' in the more or less pejorative sense in which that term can be used. Films as various as Reed's *The Fallen Idol* (1948) or *The Third Man* (1949), both from stories by Graham Greene, or Olivier's *Henry V* (1944), from Shake-speare's play, of Powell's *Black Narcissus* (1947), from Rumer Godden's novel, or John Boulting's *Brighton Rock* (1947), again from Greene, or Asquith's *The Winslow Boy* (1948), from Terence Rattigan's play, all offer distinctly cinematic experiences, their directors and screenwriters having re-imagined their literary sources in terms of what cinema could do. The Reed films in particular, like Lean's adaptations from Noël Coward (*Brief Encounter*, 1945) and Dickens (*Great Expectations*, 1946; *Oliver Twist*, 1948), all reveal as well an attachment to the realist techniques that had come to the fore in wartime British film-making. The realist is not of course the only influence at work in the aesthetic mode of such films, but it may be argued that these literary adaptations would scarcely have been made as they are in the preceding decade. Lean's depiction of Dickens's London or the provincial town in *Brief Encounter* or Reed's use of London streets in *The Fallen Idol* or of war-ravaged Vienna in *The Third Man* are key post-war examples of the fusion of the literary and the realist, however potent other interventions such as the stylistics of American *film noir*. A decade later, when the so-called British 'new wave' was winning critical plaudits, there was a new sense of realism at work on a different order of literary texts, in films such as *Room at the Top* (1959) and *Saturday Night and Sunday Morning* (1960), but the combination again won critical approval – and considerable audience support. It is not too sweeping a generalisation to say that literature-derived films with elements of physical and social realism have most often been those most closely associated with the idea of 'quality British film' which, as John Ellis has written, the critics 'passionately hoped the wide public would come to recognize and appreciate.'[5]

From its earliest days, British cinema had borrowed heavily from literary sources. So did Hollywood, but no one ever described its output as that of a 'literary cinema'. It is not just the fact of drawing on literary texts but also the kinds of sources chosen and the

[5] John Ellis, 'The Quality Film Adventure: British Critics and the Cinema, 1942–1948', in Andrew Higson (ed.), *Dissolving Views: Key Writings on British Cinema*. London: Cassell, 1996, p. 69.

strategies by which they are brought to the screen which govern the literariness or otherwise of the enterprise. What I think of as 'high' British cinema, its wonderful wartime and post-war ascendancy, was attracted notably to classics of the literature or to middle-brow, middle-class successes rather than to popular or pulp fiction in the way that Hollywood so often was. Roy Armes, British film historian, deals rather harshly with what he sees as the literary tradition in British cinema. He writes (specifically in relation to Lindsay Anderson in the 1970s) of 'the continuing gulf between writers who see them-selves primarily as novelists or playwrights merely dabbling in the cinema and directors, often with extensive stage experience, who conceive their role as that of transcribing pre-existing material into film images. The result is a notion of literary cinema which is as characteristic of British cinema as the documentary tradition'.[6] Armes makes such film production sound oddly unexciting, cer-tainly a lesser form of creativity; I shall want to argue that Lean's *Great Expectations*, seen sixty years later, escapes this particular dead hand.

Industry matters

For a brief shining hour, most of the ablest, most imaginative film-makers in Britain had what may have been idyllic working con-ditions. J. Arthur Rank, who had assumed a position of increasing dominance in British cinema since the later 1930s, established in February 1942 an umbrella organisation called Independent Producers under which would shelter the following production companies: Individual Pictures (Frank Launder and Sidney Gilliat), The Archers (Michael Powell and Emeric Pressburger), Wessex Films

---

[6] Roy Armes, *A Critical History of British Cinema*. London: Secker and Warburg, 1978, p. 277.

(Ian Dalrymple), the one-man band Gabriel Pascal, and Cineguild. The latter was set up by producer Anthony Havelock-Allan, who invited David Lean and cinematographer Ronald Neame to join him in the company that was formally constituted as Cineguild and which, in the seven years of its activity, exerted an influence out of proportion to its production output. All these companies were underwritten by Rank, who by all accounts gave his producers a remarkably free hand. Ronald Neame years later recalled: 'Now, Arthur was a wonderful man. He said to us: "Make me some good films and leave the rest to me".'[7] If this might seem like a viewing of the past through rose-tinted glasses, it is worth quoting David Lean's own comments at the time:

> I doubt if any film-makers in the world can claim as much freedom. We of Independent Producers can make any subject we wish, with as much money as we think that subject should have spent on it. We can cast whatever actors we choose, and we have no interference at all in the way the film is made … Such is the enviable position of British film-makers today, and such are the conditions which have at last given our films a style and nationality of their own.[8]

Such conditions did not last beyond the decade but, while they did, they enabled the production of some of the most distinguished films ever made in Britain to that time or since.

[7] 'Ronald Neame', in Brian McFarlane (ed.), *An Autobiography of British Cinema*. London: Methuen/BFI, 1977, p. 432.
[8] David Lean, *'Brief Encounter'*, in *Penguin Film Review*, No. 4. London and New York: Penguin, 1947.

Rank sent Neame to America to investigate technical matters to do with cinematography and when he returned he was fired by the urge to 'produce a film that might be enjoyed by American audiences ... Rank was determined to break into that market.'[9] The film he had in mind was *Great Expectations,* which he asked Lean to direct, and the resulting film did indeed have a great success in America, at least on the art-house circuit. The Cineguild outfit began to fall apart in a few years, its demise precipitated by Lean's taking over from Neame the direction of *The Passionate Friends* (1948) and by Havelock-Allan's wanting to move in other directions, but while it lasted it achieved, in Pierre Bourdieu's terms, notable symbolic and economic capital.[10] Again to cite Bourdieu, Cineguild for a few years occupied a 'dominant' position in the field of cultural production occupied by British cinema: it enjoyed high critical esteem and, in the privileged working situation provided by Rank, it had in so chancy an industry an unusual degree of economic security. It was able to be daring and the films it made exhibit notable film-makers being allowed a free hand, presumably because Rank was confident not only of the symbolic capital their films would accrue to his organisation but the economic capital that would ensue following their commercial success. As film historian James Chapman has written recently: 'For a period of four or five years in the mid-1940s, these film-makers experienced a level of both artistic and budgetary freedom that was unprecedented

---

[9] In interview with Howard Maxford. '*Great Expectations*', *Film Review*, April 2001, No. 604, p. 72.

[10] Pierre Bourdieu, *The Field of Cultural Production: Essays on Art and Literature* (edited and introduced by Randal Johnson). Cambridge: Polity Press, 1993, p. 75. The distinction is of course between works which bring critical acclaim and those which merely make a lot of money.

in British cinema. Rank was prepared to invest in 'prestige' films and to sponsor creativity and innovation.'[11]

Authorship

The question of authorship in relation to a film is always a complex one, made even more so when the film is adapted from an existing text. It is easy to say that a film is a film whether or not it has a literary ancestor; the fact is that most people will come to the film version of a classic or popular novel with some sort of preconception and (the pun is inevitable) expectation. It has become common to speak of 'Lean's *Great Expectations*'; however, not merely is there Dickens hovering over the enterprise but a battery of other crucial contributors to the film's 'authorship' too. Whereas most novels have a single author, all films are necessarily collaborative, though the collaborators are not always as distinguished as they are in this case.

Lean had a career as a prized editor in the 1930s and it is hard not to see his influence in some of the editorial decisions at work in *Great Expectations*, despite the attribution of this function to Jack Harris, who also had a long and respected record and who complained to Kay Walsh that 'he felt as though he was contributing nothing'.[12] Lean's first brush with direction was on Gabriel Pascal's *Major Barbara* (1941). Harold French was officially the director at the start, but grew so tired of Pascal's (often ignorant) interference that he 'ended up shooting the first quarter of the film ... and (editor) David Lean shot the rest of it himself, about three-

[11] James Chapman, *Past and Present: National Identity and the British Historical Film*. London: I.B. Tauris, 2005, pp. 115–16.
[12] Quoted in Kevin Brownlow, *David Lean*. London: Richard Cohen Books, 1996, p. 220.

quarters of it I suppose. Gabby took a lot of the credit but it was David mostly.'[13] When Noël Coward came to make the famous wartime hit, *In Which We Serve* (1942), he was aware of his inexperience as a film-maker, and his associate producer, Anthony Havelock-Allan, 'suggested that David Lean was the best possible person to act as technical director'.[14] These comments from Lean's colleagues suggest the kind of esteem in which, even in the early 1940s, he was held, and his star, John Mills, enthusiastically called him 'the best editor in the world, bar none', and went on to praise Lean for 'tak(ing) a book of that length and (do)ing such a masterful job of making a script which keeps the story ...'[15]

By the time Lean came to make *Great Expectations*, his reputation had risen considerably higher as a result of two further films derived from Coward plays: *This Happy Breed* (1944), a loving cavalcade of lower-middle-class British life between the wars, and *Brief Encounter* (1945), the very moving tale of middle-class near-adultery based on Coward's short play, *Still Life*. In both these films, Lean had shown his interest in realism and his capacity for taking a work created in and for another medium and rendering it in persuasive cinematic terms. But when we turn to *Great Expectations*, it has to be acknowledged that Mills's encomium elides several others who deserve major credit for the particularly 'masterful job' of which Mills spoke. Taking the example of the screenwriters, Lean shares the 'Adapted for the Screen' credit with Neame and Havelock-Allan, and there is a further writing credit which reads 'With Kay Walsh and Cecil McGivern'. (Havelock-Allan recalled Walsh and McGivern's contribution derived from their being 'very

[13] 'Harold French', in *An Autobiography of British Cinema*, p. 212.

[14] 'Anthony Havelock-Allan', op cit, p. 291.

[15] 'John Mills', op cit, p. 414.

good at dialogue'.[16]) Kay Walsh, married to Lean at the time, and unlike him a voracious reader, had introduced him to the idea of *Great Expectations* by taking him to a 1939 production of a dramatised version of the novel in the Rudolf Steiner Hall.[17] This play was the work of Alec Guinness, and starred Marius Goring as Pip (with Martita Hunt already in place as Miss Havisham, and Guinness as Herbert Pocket). Guinness recalls: 'It so happened (i.e. the result of Kay Walsh's urgings) that David Lean and Ronald Neame saw the production and decided to make a film of the book as soon as the war ended.'[18] Cecil McGivern, Controller of Television Programmes for the BBC from 1950, died in 1963, but the others lived on for several more decades (Neame at 97 is still alive at time of publication) and were clear and mutually corroborative in their recollections of the making of the screenplay. But the writing, whether of Dickens or Lean or any of the other four co-authors, is not all that is comprehended by the term of 'authorship' in relation to this – or any – film. In this case, Guy Green's Oscar-winning cinematography collaborates with John Bryan's superlative production design to recreate, not just the 'spirit' of Dickens, but a uniquely rendered feeling for time and place too. Until re-viewing the film for the purposes of this book, I had not seen it for fifteen years, and what most potently stayed in my mind was the *look* of the film, in its evocation of, say, the marshes or Satis House or Little Britain. The authorship of this film constitutes another crucially informing context for the consideration of it.

[16] 'Anthony Havelock-Allan', op cit, p. 293.

[17] Brownlow, p. 206

[18] Alec Guinness, *Blessings in Disguise* [1985]. London: Fontana Paperbacks, 1986, p. 93.

Text

Adaptation: the three stages

Like virtually all the film adaptations of *Great Expectations*, the 1946 film, in terms of running time, favours the first of the novel's three parts or 'stages', to use Dickens's word. That is, it devotes most time to the period of Pip's childhood and youth, to establishing the influences of his encounter with the convict Magwitch, the bizarre intervention of Miss Havisham and the meeting with Estella, the arrival of Mr Jaggers with his announcement of the change in Pip's fortunes, and, though he will not fully recognise its importance until near the end, the benign affection of Joe Gargery. Whereas Dickens devotes almost exactly the same number of pages to each of these stages, the filmed versions all apparently, and perhaps understandably, find it necessary to offer more expansive treatment of those incidents and characters who will exercise the most far-reaching effects on Pip. In fact, Lean's film (to lapse into authorial shorthand) is more balanced in this respect than most. Even so, it allows 43 minutes 17 seconds to the first stage, only 32 minutes 13 seconds to the second stage (Pip's London 'education' up to the return of Magwitch), and 38 minutes 37 seconds to the last (Pip's moral growth as he tries to save Magwitch). The point of these tedious statistics is to suggest that, though the film is still somewhat weighted, at least in terms of running-time, in favour of Pip's formative years, it does indicate a closer regard for Dickens's intentions, which seemed to point to the equal importance of the three stages.

Certainly, though, it is probably true to say that nothing in the rest of the film is as vivid as the rendering of the novel's first third. The film begins conventionally enough with the voice of the adult Pip (John Mills) reading on the soundtrack the opening lines of the novel as the screen is filled with its first page, but this convention quickly gives way to the wonderful images of the marsh country with the boy Pip (Anthony Wager) running to the churchyard, left to right across the screen, on an afternoon of louring clouds, high wind and a strange gleam on the water. (And in time what may have seemed an unoriginal beginning will make its point: that this is to be, as far as a film can be, a 'first-person' narrative like Dickens's own. I shall return to this.) The sound of the wind and the creaking boughs of the churchyard trees, and the visual impact of the bleak scene in which the frightened Pip, among the gravestones, is shot from angles that intensify our sense of his exposure: these create a tension that climaxes in the famously unnerving meeting with the convict Magwitch (Finlay Currie), who seizes Pip as he starts to run off. This whole opening scene offers a masterly introduction to the film at large, announcing its stylistic predilections as being at once realist *and* gothic.

The ensuing events – Pip's return to the bleakness of the forge and the Gargery kitchen; his theft of 'wittles' for Magwitch; the early morning run through the fog; the Christmas dinner; Pip's escape lunge to the doorway and its interception by the sergeant; the hunt for the convicts on the marshes; and Magwitch's recognition of Pip as having no part in his capture – are all depicted with faultless economy and a realism heightened by poetic insight. When Pip goes to the pantry, the hanging hare and the pie assume a brief accusatory life and this notion is intensified by the way Pip imagines that the cows he passes as he runs to the graveyard are rebuking him as a thief. Even the squeaking hinges of a gate join in the chorus of accusation, and this sense of guilt is important to Pip's subsequent development. As Magwitch and his fellow convict, Compeyson (George Hayes), slither round in the mud and as he is always viewed from above before disappearing in the boat, it is tempting subsequently to see Magwitch as a 'repressed' who will later 'return' with Freudian power to disrupt the tenor of the adult

Pip's life. (The American critic, James Agee, was probably the only reviewer to refer to 'the help of Freud' he detected in Lean's version of the novel.[19])

The other key encounter is that with Miss Havisham (Martita Hunt) and her ward Estella (Jean Simmons) at Satis House. This episode is brilliantly introduced by the termagant Mrs Joe (Freda Jackson) who arrives back at the forge barking orders as she dismounts from the cart: the orders, though, are rendered mutely as Lean lets the 'important' music and the editing make clear the crucial nature of what is about to happen. There is a montage of preparations (fierce scrubbings of Pip) and a grim warning from Mrs Joe who, with Pumblechook (Hay Petrie), has brought the summons from Miss Havisham who wants a boy to come to play. 'He'd better play or I'll work him,' Mrs Joe threatens with narrowed eyes. In her way, she is no more threatening to Pip than Miss Havisham will prove to be. When he arrives at Satis House, he is literally led up the garden path by Estella, as usual played as being older than Pip, who tersely encapsulates the film's concern with class by insolently referring to Pip as 'Boy', and then marches him along the passages and staircases of the gloomy house until they reach Miss Havisham's door. It is worth noting that this version of *Great Expectations* is marked by – perhaps even unified by – the images of repeated journeys, short and long. We first see Pip running along the marshes road; the journey to London is executed partly by realist shots of carriage and close-ups of Pip, partly by stylised maps; he will walk wonderingly through London streets; he will come to grief on the river as he tries to help Magwitch to escape; and the film's last image is of him and Estella running down the path to leave Satis

---

[19] James Agee, *Agee on Film*. New York: McDowell Oblonsky, 1958, p. 267 (reproduced from *Nation*, 19 July 1947).

House. At this earlier stage, though, there is a strong sense of his being led away from all he knows as he makes his way towards the confrontation with Miss Havisham.

Martita Hunt is still perhaps the definitive Miss Havisham, though as noted elsewhere in this book, the role seems to be a gift to an actress, and in adaptations of varying merits the character usually emerges with the Dickensian elements of grotesquerie and pain intact. The interiors in which she lives her reclusive days are a triumph of John Bryan's art direction, giving her the suggestion of a predatory spider in a web of dilapidation, a malign web in which both Estella and Pip are caught. While the children play 'Beggar my neighbour', she sits above and between them, the composition of the image making its point about how she manipulates them for her own reasons. On Pip's subsequent visit, the corrosively destructive power of her way of life is imaged in the decaying bridal table with the vivid detail of mice scurrying from the wedding cake. Speaking of the spectacle, she tells Pip, 'It and I have worn away together. The mice have gnawed at it and sharper teeth than teeth of mice have gnawed at me.' In these words, taken, as so much of the film's dialogue is, directly from Dickens (Ch. XI), and spoken in Hunt's resonant tones, Miss Havisham's bitterness and obsession are rendered with a flamboyance that is both riveting and affecting.

In the last of the three major confrontations of Pip's youth, Jaggers (Francis L. Sullivan) enters the forge doorway significantly coming between the shadows of the working Joe (Bernard Miles) and the now grown Pip (Mills), recalling how Miss Havisham had been placed in a similarly dominant – and disruptive – image. Jaggers has been seen before at Satis House, again placed above Pip and Estella on the stairs, so that even those unfamiliar with the book will not be surprised at how he is presented in this episode in which he conveys to Pip the news of his 'expectations'. When they move into the kitchen, Jaggers is shot from beneath in a way that reinforces his dominant role, and the camera then stays on Pip's face as he assimilates the news and what it may mean to him.

It is not possible to spend so long on how Lean (synecdoche for his whole extravagantly gifted team) renders the rest of the novel as I have on the first third. I have lingered over the latter partly because so much that happens in it is so crucial to the rest of the narrative and because almost everything in it is both Dickensian *and* a film-making triumph. The reviewer in *Monthly Film Bulletin* doesn't exaggerate when writing, 'Scenes of surpassing strength are included in the first half-hour of the film, which contains some of the finest cinema yet made in Britain'.[20] As well, the rest of the film, assured and elegant and alarming as much of it is, loses some of the wonderful freshness of observation that characterises the adaptation of the first stage. The second part of the novel, dealing with Pip's education as a gentleman, his running into debt, his frustration regarding Estella and the final return of Magwitch on the night of a wild storm, forms the basis for the shortest of the film's three main sections and there is indeed a feeling that this has not absorbed the attention of the film-makers as Pip's early years have. There is something rather rushed about Pip's arrival in London, being escorted to his rooms by Wemmick (Ivor Barnard) and meeting and recognising Herbert Pocket (Alec Guinness), who fills in the story of Miss Havisham's jilting and her plans for Estella. The processes of Pip's 'education' are collapsed into a couple of remarks on etiquette from Herbert and a somewhat conventional montage of social activities, and this montage device will be repeated later when Pip is escorting Estella (Valerie Hobson) to various London entertainments.

[20] R.M. '*Great Expectations*', *Monthly Film Bulletin*, December 1946, p.166.

The most telling scene in this section of the film is that in which Joe comes to London to bring a request from Miss Havisham for Pip to visit her. Pip, in a sleek dressing-gown, stands at the window of his rooms reading a letter from Biddy (Eileen Erskine), whose voice is heard on the soundtrack, thus placing the writing of the letter in the past. The visit is a mix of uncomfortable social comedy, as Joe behaves gauchely, and of real poignancy, as a measure of both Pip's snobbery and Joe's simple, tender perception when he explains to 'Pip, dear old chap' that 'You and me is not two figures to be together in London … I'm wrong in these clothes. I'm wrong out of the forge, the kitchen or off the marshes.' (The dialogue again is taken word for word from the novel.) The episode that concludes Dickens's second stage, the return of Magwitch, of what Pip has repressed in his social ascent, is also finely handled, in both narrative and visual terms. It begins with a glorious roof-top panning shot of the wet and stormy London night, the shot finally coming to rest on Pip's window. He is snugly within, at ease in a smoking jacket, when Magwitch appears at the doorway, in another of those bravura images in which the great influences of Pip's life are made to appear before him and us. Magwitch looms over Pip as he tells him of his experiences in New South Wales, recalling how Jaggers ('deep as Australia' in Wemmick's words) has loomed over him in the Gargery kitchen or on Miss Havisham's stairs.

The third part of the novel is inevitably concerned with a good deal of plot-unravelling but it is also, and more importantly, concerned with the loss of Pip's expectations and the resurgence of something resembling moral conscience. In all the versions of *Great Expectations*, this latter is skimped. Perhaps moral reclamation is less susceptible to the screen's visualising. Much of the final third of Lean's film is taken up with the arrangements for spiriting Magwitch out of the country and away from the reach of the law, and there is something heart-felt in the collapse of these plans, especially in the wake of a buoyant surge of music as the packet appears on the river. (It is hard to agree here with Gavin Lambert's view that, in this sequence, 'the fact that the director has no real concern with what is *happening* becomes evident.'[21]) The significance of Pip's efforts on Magwitch's behalf is noted in the latter's comment to him, as he lies in the prison infirmary, about Pip having been 'easier with me since I was under a cloud', and Pip's growth in moral stature is further rendered in his touching awareness of how unselfishly Joe has attended him in his subsequent illness. But the most potent scene in this last third of the film is that in which Pip goes to see Miss Havisham again, confronting her with the truth of his expectations and eliciting from her the great heart-sore cry of 'Who am I to be kind?' There is, too, an important exchange between Pip and Estella as the way is prepared for the film's final scene. As the hoofbeats of Drummle's carriage are heard below, she tells Pip 'I tried to tell you but you wouldn't be warned' and leaves the room to meet the boor she is engaged to marry. In the final scene, which I shall return to, Estella has been deserted by Drummle when her parentage is made known to him and she has settled herself in Miss Havisham's chair at Satis House. Lean and his writers here depart most significantly from Dickens at this point and we shall need to consider why.

Adaptation: the bones of the novel

The point of this question is not to raise the foolish and irrelevant issue of 'fidelity' in relation to adaptation, at least not as an evaluative tool. However, since this film has won such high praise and

---

[21] Gavin Lambert, 'British Films: 1947: Survey and Prospect', *Sequence Two*, Autumn 1947, p. 9.

maintained an undisputed position as the 'best' adaptation of *Great Expectations*, it may be useful to consider just how closely the screenplay has chosen to reproduce the major cardinal functions, in Barthes's terms. That is, how far has it chosen to retain those events which propose alternative outcomes, events which are linked to each other not just sequentially but *con*sequentially as well. To do so may help to focus on ways in which the film has sought to achieve the different emphases which a film-maker nearly a hundred years later might have had in mind. The following table[22] summarises the cardinal functions of the film and their relation to the film:

NOVEL	FILM
1 Pip meets Magwitch in village churchyard.	As for novel.
2 Pip steals food and file for Magwitch.	As for novel.
3 Soldiers capture Magwitch and second convict, Compeyson.	As for novel.
4 Pip visits Satis House, meets Miss Havisham and Estella.	As for novel (+ Death of Mrs Joe; Biddy's arrival).
5 Stranger at inn gives Pip a shilling wrapped in two pound notes, and stirs grog with Joe's file.	Not in film.
6 Pip returns to Satis House, meets Mr Jaggers, and fights Herbert Pocket.	As for novel.
7 Pip visits Satis House again.	Pip re-visits Satis House.

[22] This table first appeared in Brian McFarlane, *Novel to Film: An Introduction to the Theory of Adaptation*. Oxford: Clarendon Press, 1996, pp. 113–115. It is reproduced here by permission of the Oxford University Press.

NOVEL	FILM
8 Miss Havisham gives Joe £25 for Pip's indentures as blacksmith's apprentice.	Miss Havisham gives Pip money on his last visit before he goes to work. Not in film.
9 Joe takes on Orlick as journeyman worker in forge.	Not in film.
10 Pip re-visits Satis House. Estella has gone abroad.	Not in film.
11 Mrs Joe is brutally attacked (apparently with convict's leg-iron).	Not in film.
12 Biddy comes to live at the Gargery house.	See above – between 4 and 5.
13 Pip tells Biddy he wants to become a gentleman.	Ditto.
14 Jaggers brings news of Pip's 'great expectations'.	As for novel.
15 Pip goes to London.	As for novel.
16 He sets up house with Herbert Pocket at Barnard's Inn.	As for novel.
17 Herbert tells story of Miss Havisham's jilting.	As for novel.
18 Pip goes to Hammersmith, to be educated by Mr Pocket.	Not in film. (Pip's 'education' in bracket syntagma, segment 25.)
19 Pip gets money from Jaggers to set himself up.	As for novel (+ Pip and Herbert's 'At Home').
20 Pip dines with Jaggers (along with Herbert and Bentley Drummle).	Not in film.
21 Joe visits Pip at Barnard's Inn.	As for novel.
22 Pip visits Miss Havisham at her request (via Joe).	As for novel.

NOVEL	FILM
23 Pip re-meets Estella.	As for novel.
24 Pip secures Orlick's dismissal as gate-keeper at Satis House.	Not in film.
25 Pip and Herbert exchange their romantic secrets.	Not in film (Herbert's romance omitted).
26 Pip meets and escorts Estella in London.	As for the novel.
27 Pip and Herbert fall into debt.	As for novel, but earlier (after 19, above) in film.
28 Mrs Joe dies.	Much earlier in film. (See 4 above.)
29 Pip returns to village for funeral.	Long before Pip leaves village.
30 Pip's income is fixed at £500 p.a. when he comes of age.	As for novel, but before 21 (above). Not in film.
31 Pip takes Estella to Satis House.	Not in film.
32 She and Miss Havisham quarrel.	As for novel.
33 At Assembly Ball, Estella leads on Bentley Drummle.	As for novel.
34 Magwitch returns to reveal self as Pip's benefactor.	As for novel.
35 Pip verifies Magwitch's story with Jaggers.	As for novel.
36 Pip and Herbert make plans for Magwitch's escape.	Fragments of story at 34 (above) and 41 (below).
37 Magwitch tells story of his past (involving Miss Havisham and Compeyson).	As for novel.
38 Pip goes to farewell Miss Havisham and Estella.	As for novel.

	NOVEL	FILM
39	Estella tells him she is to marry Drummle.	As for novel.
40	Wemmick warns Pip of being watched.	As for novel.
41	Pip, with help of Herbert and Wemmick, makes further plans for Magwitch's escape.	Not in film.
42	Pip visits Satis House to ask Miss Havisham to finance Herbert.	Not in film.
43	Pip tries to save Miss Havisham from burning.	As for novel, but combined with 38–39 (above).
44	Jaggers (reluctantly) tells Pip Estella's true story.	As for novel, but not until after 50 (below).
45	Pip goes to deserted sluice house.	Not in film.
46	Pip is saved from death at Orlick's hand by arrival of Herbert and others at sluice house.	Not in film.
47	The escape plan for Magwitch fails.	As for novel.
48	Pip loses fortune.	As for novel.
49	Magwitch is tried.	As for novel.
50	Magwitch dies in prison.	As for novel.
51	Pip becomes ill.	As for novel.
52	Joe looks after Pip.	As for novel.
53	Biddy and Joe get married.	Not clear when marriage has occurred.
54	Pip re-meets Estella in the ruins of Satis House.	As for novel but with altered circumstances and outcome.

Though some may contend for other events as having the status of cardinal functions, I would claim only that each of those fifty-four listed above is important for its causal connection to what follows. It could be argued that the film, in doing away with, say, Mr Wopsle's career on the London stage, is then forced to omit the sighting of the returned convict Compeyson. Nevertheless, everything listed above does act as a hinge-point of narrative, when there are alternative possibilities for what ensues. Such a table of course pays no attention to all the cinematic means by which these events are rendered; it simply makes clear the extent to which the film has retained the skeleton of the original narrative. Indeed, one reviewer at the time of the film's release wrote that 'Every bone of the original comes through as if it were seen by an x-ray'.[23]

Adaptation: omissions and changes

It is inevitable that, in adapting a long, complex novel to produce a two-hour film, the film-makers will have to make serious choices about what to leave out. When the Cineguild team came to make *Oliver Twist* two years later, they acted more ruthlessly in this respect, ditching the entire slab of the novel in which Oliver fetches up with the Maylie family and is consequently missing from the central action of the novel. The film keeps him there right up to his rooftop rescue and restoration to Mr Brownlow. It is arguably an improvement on the novel's procedures, and it is also arguably a more rigorous job of adaptation than is on display in *Great Expectations*. After the vividly detailed first third, there is some sense of 'shaving' down the novel rather than opting for the draconian excisions of *Oliver Twist* (or, more recently, of Hossein Amini's screenplay for *The Wings of the Dove*, 1997, in which the focus is unrelentingly on the

[23] C.A. Lejeune, *Observer*, 15 December 1946.

central trio). In this respect, the film scarcely needs Wemmick's Aged P. (O.B. Clarence) who is there for a few moments and a nod or two. The whole business of Pip's London education, of his becoming a 'fine gentleman', of his jealousy of Bontley Drummle, of his running into debt is somewhat breathlessly accomplished in a couple of montages which are visually striking enough but not very satisfying in terms of what they are meant to be revealing about Pip.

The omissions that interest me particularly are those that are common to all the film versions of the novel: that is, Orlick, Wopsle and Trabb's boy. Two of the television versions previously discussed retain Orlick and, I think, benefit by doing so. Orlick is the journey-man in Joe's forge who is, from his first appearance there, resentful of what he sees as Pip's superior status as apprentice. Unlike Pip, Orlick will never have any great expectations; his life will be one of sulky frustration and rage; and his murder of Mrs Joe intensifies Pip's sense of guilt attaching to himself. Trabb's boy, on the other hand, is the provincial boy who is quite at home with himself. His antennae for delusion and affectation are finely, and good-humouredly, attuned. He has no expectations either, but has not been soured by the limitations of his life. Wopsle has a go in the big city, but the one instance of his thespian aspiration that we see does not bode well for his taking the capital by storm, even should it be 'thrown open'. Now, the events associated with these three can be omitted without obscuring Pip's main line of development but what the film does miss as a result is a thinning out of its perception of Pip. By contrast with the grotesques who cross his path, Pip is a comparatively shadowy figure, but the novel reinforces the reader's appreciation of what, for good and ill, happens to him by the implied comparisons and contrasts with these three other figures. There are, of course, other comparisons that do some of the work, most notably that with Estella as much a product of arbitrary influences as Pip himself, though the film omits her quarrel with Miss Havisham. Herbert, with his very limited prospects, is played with great charm by Alec Guinness but neither his romance nor his modest business success is alluded to and his dramatic value as comparative figure is diminished. And Drummle is there, if perfunctorily so: Torin Thatcher has a fine sneering way with his lines, but they are too few to articulate the interesting contrast of another young man who has nothing *but* expectations and whose character has been corrupted by them. It is perhaps the result of such omissions that the second and third stages of Pip's expectations are less rich and rewarding than the first: they need, as the first did not, the commentative texture of these other lives to bolster our sense of Pip as a substantial protagonist. In none of the foregoing am I arguing a case for fidelity to the original: rather, I want to suggest that some means might have been found to achieve a more complex figure at the centre of the action.

There may be several such omissions but the film 'changes' very little in the matter of events and the perspectives from which they are viewed. The ending constitutes one important exception. As every writer on the film has noted, Lean has opted for a much more consciously upbeat ending than Dickens. It is well-known that Dickens changed his original ending – a chance meeting between Pip and Estella in Piccadilly with no suggestion of any lasting reunion – on the suggestion of his friend Bulwer Lytton. As a result the published ending, sombre, subdued, set in what remains of the gardens of Satis House, seems to catch just the merest possibility of at least, in Estella's words, 'continu(ing) friends apart':

I took her hand in mine, and we went out of the ruined place; and, as the morning mists had risen long ago when I first left the forge, so, the evening mists were rising now, and in all the broad expanse of tranquil light they showed to me, I saw no shadow of another parting from her.

It may be argued that films very often, in the interests of widespread popularity, tend to have happier endings than novels. In this case, it is also possible to mount another case for the film ending as it does: that is, this is a film made in the year after a long hard war has finished, in a period when a new Labour government has ousted the Churchillian wartime coalition. There were expectations of a new sort of equality, of a doing away with the dusty outmoded traditions that had relegated some sectors of society to the ranks of the underprivileged – even, of the oppressed.

First, think of Magwitch from this 1946 point of view. The return of Magwitch, last seen shackled and well below the watching Pip, Joe and the others, appears later in the dominant image of the revenant towering over Pip in his London doorway. We can read the film as a socio-political document in which the long-repressed under-classes (represented by Magwitch slithering in the mud) return to assert themselves against the forces that have kept them down. Pip thus becomes the instrument of Magwitch's revenge: he has 'made' Pip into the sort of gentleman who has hounded and betrayed him. Well, Magwitch is betrayed again by the gentleman convict Compeyson and Pip's effort to rescue him fails. In 1946 it is conceivable that such a muted ending as the Satis House garden meeting might simply have seemed too lacking in buoyancy. If Magwitch's efforts, however misguided, are to have meant any-thing, something needs to have been salvaged.

Lean has Pip return to Satis House, to find Estella (as noted above) installed in Miss Havisham's old chair, and her having adopted the same position as her late guardian, opting for the same reclusiveness, suggests that, in spite of all that has gone before, nothing has changed. It is as though Pip, having failed to save Magwitch, the great agent of change in his life, must not allow this situation of stasis to continue. Satis House, not destroyed as in the novel, is now no more than an airless relic of the past, of a past in which lives were cruelly manipulated. Pip, returning to Satis House, recalls the sound of the young Estella's voice and of Miss Havisham's dismissing 'the days of the week or the months of the year', as he retakes his 'journey' into the house and up the stairs. But this Pip, so little an agent in the conduct of his earlier life, is now a more forceful figure: like the nation battered by war, he has survived, and he now takes the initiative. 'You must leave this house. It's a dead house,' he insists to her. He 'defies' Miss Havisham and what she stood for – for stasis and decay and manipulation. 'Come with me out into the sunlight' he urges. 'We belong to each other – let's start together again'. And they run down the same garden path by which he'd first approached Satis House. That last line of dialogue smacks of cinema-romantic, but it reminds us that there is more at stake in this ending than either Dickens or 1946: this is a film which, it was hoped, would appeal widely, that is, as Hollywood-habituated audiences might have expected. The hero, then, might be expected to be more proactive than Dickens's Pip, the reconciliation a little more explicitly optimistic, a point of view emphasised by the superimposition over the final image not of the expected words THE END but, instead, GREAT EXPECTATIONS. For another point of view, one critical account of the ending has this to say: 'Finally, there is the latent irony in the superimposed "Great Expectation" for the future may be only that, expectations without fulfilment, and nothing more. Many questions are never resolved ... traces of ambiguity linger over the film as a whole'.[24]

[24] Alain Silver and James Ursini, *David Lean and His Films*. Los Angeles: Silman-James Press, 1992, p. 67.

This change of tone and indeed of action in the film's last sequence not only seems in line with the film's production period of post-war hopefulness, or with its need to bolster the leading man's role in accordance with popular taste, but it also underscores the story's affiliations with tho fairy talo. In tho functional torms analyzed by Propp in his study of Russian folk tales,[25] Pip is the hero whose quest for the grail of gentility and that of love has been hindered and advanced in varying measure by those he meets along his path, from the graveyard at the novel and film's start to Satis House at the end, the ruined garden in the novel, the musty neglected house in the film. Seen in this light, it is clear that some, like Joe and Herbert, perform the roles of helper, Magwitch is both donor and, in a limited way that will be called into question, also something of a helper, while others like Drummle and Compeyson are clearly villains, obstructions to the achievements of Pip's goals. Miss Havisham is in some obvious ways a donor, but her function is clearly not wholly benign; there is something of the bad fairy in her, hovering over the lives of the innocent young. The comparison between her and Magwitch is instructive in this respect. I have written elsewhere that: 'The fairy godmother in the drama of Pip's career is revealed as being nearer to the ogre who inhibits it, a function which Magwitch at first appears to fulfil, whereas his intentions are later revealed as benign if misguided.'[26] Lean was on record as saying that 'part of our intention was to make a fairy tale':[27] the material is there in the original with such elements as an

[25] V. Propp, *Morphology of the Folktale* (1928), trans. Laurence Scott. Austin: University of Texas Press, 1968.

[26] McFarlane, *Novel to Film*, p. 118.

[27] Quoted by C.A. Lejeune, 'Communiqués from the London film front', *New York Times*, 29 June 1947, section 2, p. 5.

anonymous legacy, mysterious parentage, the whole apparatus of the advancing and thwarting of the hero's aspirations. It is not then surprising that the film-makers should have decided to include the clinching fairy-tale element by allowing the prince finally to win the elusive princess.

For Valerie Hobson, the film's more upbeat ending was a matter of the 'two young people going from the darkness into the light, away from all the nonsense and evil that had gone on over the years',[28] an assessment that seems to bear out the 'fairy-tale' aspect of the director's intentions. The reasons for this notably different approach to the last encounter of the film may well be a combination of aesthetic, ideological and commercial: they remain speculative: what matters is how satisfying and coherent a conclusion the episode offers to the film as a whole. There is at very least a pleasing symmetry in the way the film begins with the boy running across the marshes to the graveyard and ends with him running down the pathway of, and away from, the house that has changed his life. There is a sense of a life still in motion, of the possibility of lessons having been learnt, of more profoundly valuable expectations awaiting the life-chastened pair. In the light of the foregoing, I can't accept this recent denunciation of the ending: 'Notoriously, the Lean ending is banal and unconvincing, a wet spot the viewer wants to avoid rolling onto once the best parts of the film are over.'[29] Perhaps there is always a touch of the banal about happiness; certainly there is more interest to this finale than the quoted comment allows.

[28] 'Valerie Hobson', in *An Autobiography of British Cinema*, p. 304.
[29] Regina Barreca, 'David Lean's *Great Expectations*', in John Glavin (ed) *Dickens on Screen*. Cambridge: Cambridge University Press, 2003, p. 39.

Pip's voice and how it makes itself heard

One of the most striking aspects of the novel is the author's control of the narrating voice of Pip. From that first moment in the graveyard to the last reflection on the possible future for him and Estella, everything we know is filtered through Pip's first person narration. This 'voice' is inevitably more mature, more perceptive, more ironical than the Pip whose behaviour is being described. Film does not in general have much truck with extended first-person narration. Plenty of films will begin with a voice-over to draw us into their worlds: private-eye films of the 1940s quite commonly did so, but so did romantic melodramas such as *Rebecca* (1940) and *Random Harvest* (1942); few, however, took it as far as Robert Montgomery did in his adaptation of *The Lady in the Lake* (1946), as near to a first-person film as we can imagine, and almost never imitated, with the protagonist never seen unless, say, reflected in a mirror but much heard in voice-over. In more recent times, voice-over, though not in the first-person mode, was more pervasively used in Martin Scorsese's *The Age of Innocence* (1993) than perhaps ever before. Lean has not sought to emulate in *Great Expectations* the approach taken by either Montgomery in the same year or Scorsese nearly fifty years later, yet, I would maintain, he has succeeded entirely in keeping Pip at the centre of the film. Incidentally, it is worth noting that the 'book of the film' which came out in 1946 'to provide the film-going public with a record of an outstanding film which they have enjoyed and loved' does away with the first-person narration and it is remarkable how flat it seems in consequence.[30]

---

[30] *Great Expectations: The Book of the Film*, based on the novel by Charles Dickens. London: World Film Publications Ltd, 1946, p. 5.

Voice-over is only the most obvious cinematic equivalent of the novelist's first-person narration. Lean uses it sparingly. Pip's voice is heard on the soundtrack in the opening image of the novel's pages as he reads about his younger self shivering by the graves of his late parents and siblings. Cunningly, the voice is that of the mature Pip, John Mills, whose reading voice then contemplates the running figure of his young self, played by Anthony Wager. It could be argued that this is a way of announcing the film's trajectory: the running boy's career will occupy us until he has reached the insights of the voice that introduces him. The older Pip thus 'pictures' the younger version of himself just as the film's image pictures the verbal account of its opening page. Elsewhere, the voice-over device is used to announce the passing of time ('Three months later my sister became ill and was laid to rest in the village churchyard'; 'My boyhood had ended and my life as a blacksmith had begun ...'), or to spell out Pip's growing feeling for Estella ('My admiration for her knew no bounds and scarce a night went by without my falling asleep with the image of her pretty face before my eyes', spoken by the grown Pip over the image of the boy lying in bed) or for self-appraisal. The most striking example of the latter is in the scene in which Joe visits Pip in London. As Pip observes the approach of Joe stiffly attired in his Sunday best, his older self recalls on the soundtrack what his feelings had been: 'Let me confess. If I could have kept him away by paying money, I would certainly have paid money. In trying to become a gentleman, I had succeeded in becoming a snob.' The central sentence of those three is taken directly from Chapter XXVII; the final one is the film's gesture towards thematic explicitness, but the voice-over also serves the purpose of retaining some sympathy for Pip. That is, he may be a snob in regard to Joe's arrival, but the voice-over implies that at some future time he has been aware of this failing and outgrown it: the 'snobbery' belongs to the visual image of the young man in the dressing-gown looking down to the street below; the voice to some undefined future time. The disjunction of the visual and the aural at this point is important to the project of keeping the audience on side with Pip, despite his moral growing pains.

But voice-over is not the only, or even the most potent, means by which Lean keeps Pip at the centre of the narrative. Some years ago I argued in an essay that there are at least three other crucial ways in which Pip's centrality is achieved: they are in the near omnipresence of Pip in the film's action; the high level of subjective camera-work that compels us to share Pip's literal and, by extension, metaphorical – point of view; and the composition of screen space so often at the service of securing our sympathetic alignment with Pip.[31] It is these, rather than the necessarily inter-mittent voice-over, which do the work of the novel's narrating voice and its obvious control over what we know. As to the idea of his near-omnipresence, there are scarcely any scenes, or even parts of scenes, when Pip is not physically present; if he was not present at the time (as when Herbert goes to the steamship office to buy tickets for Magwitch's escape) it is made clear by the voice-over that Pip is aware of what is going on. There is a shot of Compeyson observing the activity on the river in preparation for the escape, a presence that Pip has no knowledge of but which the audience needs to be able to grasp how the escape plan is later foiled. Establishing shots of, say, the forge and the attached cottage, or the dome of St Paul's Cathedral, are clearly from Pip's point of view, the latter especially vivid as a kind of metonymy for all that

31 Brian McFarlane, 'David Lean's *Great Expectations*: Meeting Two Challenges', *Literature/Film Quarterly*, Vol. 20, No. 1, 1992, pp 70–73.

London may hold for the aspiring young man. So many scenes are initiated by Pip's arrival somewhere (the churchyard, the forge, Satis House, London, etc) or begun by shots of him (dancing with a chair, uneasy at Barnard's Inn on the night of Magwitch's return, lying in the grass as he talks to Joe and Biddy in the penultimate sequence), that it seems safe to say that Lean has felt a real need to keep Pip as the pivot on which the narrative turns. If he is not the agent of change, he is the one on whom changes are repeatedly wrought. In the matter of composition, I have already indicated above some of the moments in which our sympathetic attention is drawn to Pip as a result of his being towered over by threatening figures: the convict looming over him; Mrs Joe applying 'Tickler' to his backside; his being talked over at the Christmas dinner table; Jaggers, on the stairs above him at Satis House, delivering his opinion about boys ('you're a bad set of fellows'); the return of Magwitch. In all these instances, Pip is seen at a spatial disadvantage in relation to the other characters, so that our involvement with him retains its sympathetic colouring. The great exception in this regard is in the moment discussed above when Pip, from the height of his window and his snobbery, observes the approach of Joe. The composition here reflects by contrast his moral nadir.

Compared with the cinematically unimaginative renderings in the 1934 and 1975 versions, Lean's film again and again suggests the work of a film-maker who knows how to make the screen's strategies work for him. Pip is not the sort of protagonist who makes things happen; rather, things happen to *him*. Nevertheless, even if he is surrounded by characters intrinsically more flamboyant or more idiosyncratic or more vivid in some other way than he, it is crucial to the drama of his moral education that he maintains his grip on our interest and sympathy. The matters in which he does act – his attempt to rescue Miss Havisham from the fire; the escape plan for Magwitch – end in failure. Yet, by the end of the film, he needs to be seen to have profited in terms of character and is finally allowed the great defiant gesture of tearing down the ruined curtains of Satis House, letting the light in and reclaiming Estella for life rather than the death-in-life to which she has consigned herself. The Pip whom Lean has kept at the centre of our attention, however clamorous others are for that at certain moments, is rewarded by being given moments of vigorous initiative at the end of a story in which he has so often been seen to be put upon and used.

PART THREE:

The afterlife of Lean's film

a film of its time – and for other times

··

Lean's *Great Expectations* is an example of British prestige film-making, from a prestige company, at a time when British films were enjoying, albeit briefly, a period of high international esteem. Where essentially does the film's distinction lie? Some of the answers to this question have been hinted at earlier. For instance, in the way that Lean and his Cineguild team embrace the representational mode of realism, valorised by so much British film-making and apply it to the adaptation of an author with whom realism is not the first descriptor that comes to mind. And yet, Lean's *Great Expectations* does not offer that subdued grey restraint that is often associated with British film realism. Significantly, Robert Krasker was dismissed as cinematographer because Lean wanted something 'much more daring, huge great black shadows, great big highlights – over the top'.[1] It is as though the film-makers have grasped that to be true to this world of cruelty and contrasting virtues something more than a documentary look is required. There is no faulting the precision with which details of forge and kitchen and marshes are realised; nor of the more fantastical interiors of Satis House or of the

[1] Quoted in Brownlow, p. 213.

streets of London or the bleak expanses of the river. But it is a precision which does not disdain those touches of the gothic that heighten the realist images and provide a visual analogy with Dickens's vividly imaginative prose. The child Pip's run through the morning fog is recorded as a 'real' run but its terrors are intensified by his guilty imaginings which Lean renders through the visual and aural images of cows and gates that seem to talk. (Critic C.A. Lejeune took exception to cows' mouthing Pip's guilt: 'This is not art; this is nonsense.'[2]) The shrouded whiteness of Miss Havisham's retreat and the cobwebby disorder of the bridal table are created in realist detail but resonate metaphorically beyond their material presences: they are shot in such ways as to encapsulate the concept of the ruinous decay that has followed the woman's life-denying seclusion.

The film's visual power has been referred to in several places above. It needs emphasising because it has been a recurring criticism of British cinema that it was too often over-verbal at the expense of the visual. 'Photographs of people talking', as Karel Reisz once said.[3] The criticism was probably never as wholly deserved as the detractors of British cinema would have it; it was certainly not true of the best of 1940s British films, including not only the critically privileged work of Lean, or Michael Powell, or Carol Reed, but also of the Gainsborough melodramas which only the public then knew how to value. Lean, who came rapidly to the height of his powers in the 1940s, had on *Great Expectations* an exceptionally gifted team of collaborators. The gleaming chiaroscuro of Oscar-winning Guy Green's cinematography seems made for the powerful contrasts of Dickens, and for Lean's version of

[2] C.A. Lejeune, *The Observer*, 18 December 1946.

[3] Interview with Karel Reisz, London, 1992.

Dickens, and John Bryan's design (he had also worked for Gains-borough, notably responsible for the sumptuous evocation of Victorian London in its *Fanny by Gaslight*, 1994) is a major component in the film's masterly blend of the realist and the gothic.

The more we consider that last phrase - 'blend of the realist and the gothic' - the more aptly it seems to account for the film at large. It certainly encompasses the performances. John Mills's adult Pip is a strong, careful, intelligent reading of the largely reactive protagonist's role; the *New York Times* critic went so far as to say that 'Pip actually has more stature here than in the book'.[4] Valerie Hobson's Estella has probably been undervalued because of its contrast with the vividness of Jean Simmons as the young Estella. That may well be to miss the point: the irresistibly vivacious insolence of the young Estella has been educated out of the grown woman and Hobson registers this sense of emotional lacuna with dignity and indeed some poignancy. Hobson herself understood this situation: 'When you see Estella "grown up", you feel this vivacity has been suppressed, and I think this suited my particular style very well.'[5] These two characters, more or less in the realist mode, and seen to have grown from their younger selves, are surrounded by a bevy of larger-than-life types: the gauchely benign Joe (Bernard Miles), the bullying Mrs Joe (Freda Jackson, the great harridan of British films), the farouche Magwitch (Finlay Currie, whose imposing stature looms over Mills as his character looms over Pip's life), the bizarre Miss Havisham (Martita Hunt, synonymous with eccentricity in British cinema of the period), the overbearing Jaggers (Francis L. Sullivan, who had rehearsed the role in the 1934 US version), the clerk Wemmick who keeps his domestic life secret (the austere-

[4] Bosley Crowther, *The New York Times*, 23 May 1947.
[5] 'Valerie Hobson', *An Autobiography of British Cinema*, p. 305.

looking Ivor Barnard), the arch-hypocrite Pumblechook (Hay Petrie), and those fleeting glimpses of the Christmas dinner guests and the sycophants who hover round Miss Havisham. Assisted by dialogue which is very often taken from the novel, these actors not merely evoke Dickens in themselves, but perform the dramatic task of contrast with the more realistically conceived young people. The contemporary reviewer, Richard Winnington, found that in the film, 'the acceptable adjustment between the realism of the camera and Dickens's robust enlargement of character is made.'[6] No other Dickens adaptation, with the possible exception of Lean's own *Oliver Twist* (1948) or George Cukor's *David Copperfield* (1935), has so vivified the Dickensian caricatures which the reader has believed in on the page because of the sheer intensity with which they have been imagined.

The film then is a product of its times, both of its film-making period and of the socio-political realities of its period, as well as being a handsomely intelligent adaptation of a well-loved novel. It is interesting, now, to consider how it was received in its time and how its reputation has been sustained or modified since.

Reception
Then...

The trade papers were generally ecstatic about the film's prospects. The recurring tenor of their comments was that the Cineguild team had, in the words of *Kinematograph Weekly*, made a film that was not only a masterpiece of its type, but an infallible box-office proposition.[7] There was stress on what a clever adaptation it was: the *Motion Picture Herald* praised the 'artful

[6] Richard Winnington, *News Chronicle*, 11 December 1946.
[7] Anon., *Kinematograph Weekly*, 12 December 1946, p. 20.

compressing into two hours' time of Dickens' rambling novel'[8] at the time of its New York opening, and an earlier reviewer in the same journal, reporting from the London opening, began his review with: 'There will be many who will hail this as Britain's most memorable contribution in her most memorable motion picture year to date.'[9] *Today's Cinema* considered it a 'Superlative British screen achievement assured of delighted reception by every English-speaking patron.'[10] Much was made of the excellence of the acting by the 'host of colourful and lifelike characters' (*Kine Weekly*), the attention to recreating 'the frills and furbelows of the 19th century's earliest years, the robust raffishness of Dickens' London ... displayed with impeccable skill to the vast delight of the beholder and the considerable profit of the theatre operator'.[11] The trade papers were at pains to show their appreciation of the film as a 'work of art',[12] as well as rubbing their hands at the certainty of a healthy box-office. Interestingly, in the light of Ronald Neame's avowed aim (see the previous chapter) of producing a film that would do well in the US, the two *Motion Picture Herald* reviews raise this matter. The earlier one claims enthusiastically that 'It's a peach of a picture, which cries aloud for early American exhibition', while the later one, after the New York première, considers that 'Because of (its) restraint, and because of the relatively unknown leads, this picture will take some special handling', though hoping that the fact of its having opened at the widely known Radio City Music Hall would help its prospects.

[8] R.L., *Motion Picture Herald*, 29 March 1947, p. 3549.
[9] Peter Burnup, *Motion Picture Herald*, 28 December 1946, p. 3385.
[10] C.A.W., *Today's Cinema*, 12 December 1946.
[11] Burnup, op cit.
[12] *Kinematograph Weekly*, op cit, p. 22.

The newspaper reviews in the main echoed the panegyrics of the trade press, albeit in more considered tones. Two of the most influential British reviewers of the day were Dilys Powell and Richard Winnington, writing respectively for the *Sunday Times* and the *News Chronicle*, and both, despite some reservations, wrote warmly about the film. Powell, while careful to distance herself from the slipshod 'fidelity' school of adaptation criticism, considers this 'exceptionally well-made film first of all as a piece of cinema, and second only as a version of a work in another medium.'[13] However, she does have some minor quibbles about missing characters (Trabb's boy is most writers' noted omission) and suggests that the 'camera could have strengthened the necessarily abbreviated dialogue'. Finally, though, she is 'grateful for cinema which includes so much of Dickens, which constructs its narrative from the original material with scarcely an intrusion'. Winnington, offering the opinion that 'Dickens has never before been rendered effectively into cinema terms', ends by echoing the trade press when he writes: '*Great Expectations* is a lavish, unostentatious film, romantic, exciting and English to the core. It will have, I venture to prophecy (*sic*), the best of all Box-Office worlds.'[14] *The Star* continued the common double-barrelled praise: 'This film of a great novel misses nothing of its essential spirit ... (and) is a triumph of British film-making'.[15] The left-leaning *Tribune* echoed these sentiments, praising the film for 'endowing Dickens' printed words with visual form, life and atmosphere', claiming that the film 'will do more than any other studio product to heighten the prestige of our industry in

[13] Dilys Powell, *Sunday Times*, December 1946 (reprinted in George Perry (ed), *The Golden Screen*. London: Pavilion Books, 1989, p. 63).

[14] Winnington, op cit.

[15] A.E. Wilson, 'Valerie Hobson as Dickens beauty', *The Star*, 13 December 1946.

this country and abroad.'[16] John Ross in the *Daily Worker*, praising it as 'one of the very best films made for years', felt that it would 'give vast pleasure to most people, Dickensians and others' and that it was the sort of film 'that Hollywood would dearly love to make'.[17] One of the few even mildly dissentient notes was struck by Campbell Dixon in the *Daily Telegraph*, but his reservations were chiefly attributed to what he believed to be Dickens's unreal characters and contrived plotting, asserting that 'as a transcript of a novel it is faultless, or as near as makes no matter'. As a 'mirror to life', however, it is constrained by Dickens's shortcomings and the result, though 'there are fine things in it', is 'an entertaining hotchpotch of genius and fudge.'[18] C.A. Lejeune, less ready to impugn Dickens's plotting and characterisation, still felt that the film 'falls only where Dickens fails', by which she means that neither he nor the film sustains 'the wonderful atmosphere of the opening chapters'.[19] Such quibbles, though, hardly dented the over-all reception or the effect of such comments as Stephen Watts's in the *Daily Express*: 'Britain makes her greatest film'.[20]

The point of adducing these immediate responses to the film is to draw attention to the twin preoccupations with the film's dealings with Dickens and with the prestige it was likely to bring to the British film industry. As to the former, despite Dilys Powell's disclaimer, virtually all the reviewers explicitly comment on what the film has included and/or omitted from the novel, at least implicitly commending the film for its Dickensian qualities. Equally, though,

16 *Tribune*, 12 December 1946 (BFI files, author's name not given).

17 John Ross, *Daily Worker*, 14 December 1946.

18 Campbell Dixon, *Daily Telegraph*, 16 December 1946.

19 C.A. Lejeune, *The Observer*, 18 December 1946.

20 Stephen Watts, *Daily Express*, 15 December 1946.

there is a sort of patriotic pride in the film's being a British achievement, and an awareness of its place in this palmy period of British film-making. The specialist journal *Monthly Film Bulletin,* finding much to praise in the deployment of `the visual power of the cinema to make the many dramatic situations in the story vivid', concludes with `*Great Expectations* is a unique and reassuring British film.'[21] In Britain itself, one of the least laudatory accounts of the film was given by Gavin Lambert in the short-lived but, as time has shown, influential magazine, *Sequence*: `One feels that it is not so much an attempt to recreate Dickens on the screen, as a very graceful evasion of most of the issues.'[22] But this report came nine months later, by which time the film had won golden opinions across the spectrum of press and journals at home and was finding similar favour in America.

Over there ...

As English reviewers were quick to note, especially those in the trade papers, success in America was vital. Bosley Crowther, long-time critic for *The New York Times*, rhapsodised: `For here, in a perfect motion picture, made in England (where it should have been made), the British have done for Dickens what they did for Shakespeare with Henry V: they have proved that his works have more life in them than almost anything now written for the screen.'[23] He believes that `the picture is so truly Dickens ... that the quality of the author is revealed in every line'. Writing in *Nation,* James Agee opened his review with an echo of Crowther: `*Great Expectations* does for Dickens about what *Henry V* did for Shakespeare. That is,

[21] R.M., op cit.

[22] Lambert, op cit.

[23] Crowther, op cit.

it indicates a sound method for translating him from print to film.'[24]
He goes on to praise the film as 'almost never less than graceful,
tasteful, and intelligent', adding 'and some of it is better than that'
but takes issue with those 'many people (who) feel that Great
Expectations is about as good a job as the screen can do'.[25] Time
magazine took up the comparison with Henry V: 'In Henry V,
Laurence Olivier and his British associates showed for the first time
how beautifully Shakespeare can be brought to the screen. In
Great Expectations, Britain's director David Lean (rhymes with
keen) and associates have done just as handsomely by Charles
Dickens.'[26] And Theatre Arts completed its review by noting that:
'Great Expectations breaks precedent by being the first English film
to enter the hallowed confines of Radio City Music Hall. It should fill
those precincts with delight'.[27] Much had been made in the English
press about this auspicious US launch-pad, and producer Ronald
Neame who had initiated the film's making must have felt hopeful
that he had indeed made a film which would work across the
Atlantic. Nevertheless, though it was always next to impossible to
get reliable figures on American audiences for British films, Neame,
talking about the matter over forty years later, said: 'The American
market liked Great Expectations very much, but of course it was
still an art-house film, as all ours were ... (It) cost only about £375,000
but it was too much for what we were receiving back. We needed
a world market and we needed America'.[28] If it did not take middle
America by storm, it performed well in the still-lucrative art-house

[24] Agee, op cit.
[25] Agee, p. 268.
[26] Time Magazine, May 1947.
[27] Theatre Arts, Vol xxxi, No 6, June 1947, p. 49.
[28] 'Ronald Neame', An Autobiography of British Cinema, p.432.

market and in college towns. It also won two Oscars, not in those days lightly given to British films: for Guy Green's cinematography (he, as noted, had replaced Robert Krasker early in the filming, Krasker having shot the opening sequence[29]) and for John Bryan and Wilfred Shingleton's art direction.

Later ...

In the decades that have followed the film's release, it has been much written about and its director David Lean has been the subject of several critical books and a magisterial biography by film historian Kevin Brownlow. The latter gives the most fascinating account of the film's production, drawing on the recollections of Lean himself and of collaborators still living at the time, including Anthony Havelock-Allan and his then-wife Valerie Hobson. Though Brownlow speaks of how 'Dickens' brilliance at creating characters was matched by Cineguild's choice of actors',[30] citing the gallery of memorable performances (Hunt, Sullivan, etc), he also quotes Hobson's unhappy memories of playing Estella: 'But he was such a cold director. He gave me nothing at all as an actress'. As suggested above, her performance may well have been undervalued, in that she does contrive to create a credible figure out of one of Dickens's least fully imagined characters; it is, though, a curious and provocative comment about a director who made his name in adaptation of one of the least cold, least restrained of British authors. Further insight into the film's production history, including some of the tensions generated by Lean's working habits, and into some of the influences on its design style are given in *David Lean*, a hand-

[29] Douglas Bankston, 'Wrap Shot', *American Cinematographer*, March 2000, p. 136.

[30] Brownlow, op cit, p. 211.

some volume by Stephen M. Silverman.[31] Lean seems to have been a figure who divides people, both in their reactions to him as a man and in critical response to his *oeuvre*. But in relation to *Great Expectations* there is an unusual degree of consensus in the writing, both at the time of its production and later. There are valuable later critical commentaries on the film, notably from Alain Silver and James Ursini, who rightly draw attention to the film's 'overall narrative subjectivity', finding Lean 'more than faithful to the original's first person style'.[32] There are any number of critical articles which focus on the film as an adaptation,[33] as a film reflecting social and cultural history,[34] or in comparison with other, later adaptations.[35]

The film continues to stimulate discussion and its critical status has generally stayed high, even though Lean's reputation, in the wake of the wildly over-long, over-elaborate *Dr Zhivago* (1965) and *Ryan's Daughter* (1970) (and only partially retrieved by *A Passage to India*, 1984), is perhaps not what it was. In his later films, some would even include *Lawrence of Arabia* (1962) in such a criticism: he succumbed to a pictorialism that blunted those effects of character and clean, swift story-telling which characterised his style in the period of *Great Expectations*. Be that as it may, this 1946 film has become something of a bench-mark in the filming of the

[31] Stephen M. Silverman, *David Lean*. London: André Deutsch, 1989.

[32] Silver and Ursini, op cit, p. 52.

[33] See Brian McFarlane, 'David Lean's *Great Expectations* – Meeting Two Challenges' and Guerric DeBona, 'Doing Time; Undoing Time: Plot Mutation in David Lean's *Great Expectations*, both in *Literature/Film Quarterly*, Vol. 20, No. 1, 1991.

[34] David Lusted, 'Literary Adaptations and Cultural Fantasies', *Journal of Popular British Cinema*, No. 4, 2001.

[35] Michael K. Johnson, 'Not Telling the Story the Way It Happened: Alfonso Cuarón *Great Expectations*, *Literature/Film Quarterly*, Vol. 33, No. 1.

classics. It has joined its literary antecedent as a hypotext which is taken into the reckoning whenever a new version of the novel is mounted or maybe even when a new version of *any* classic novel is considered. In 1999, it was voted fifth most admired British film ever by 1000 leading industry figures in a poll conducted by the BFI. second and third places were occupied by *Brief Encounter* and *Lawrence of Arabia*, so perhaps Lean's reputation, at least at home, is more secure than I have suggested above. For a black-and-white film made sixty years ago, *Great Expectations* seems to be holding its own.

select bibliography

....

NB The following list does not contain references to newspaper reviews; these are cited in the notes as they occur in the text. The books and articles below may provide useful further reading; they do not constitute an exhaustive list of all the works consulted or cited. As far as the films are concerned, there is little sustained writing about any of the adaptations other than Lean's.

Agee, James. *Agee on Film*. New York: McDowell Oblornsky, 1958.

Armes, Roy. *A Critical History of British Cinema*. London: Secker and Warburg, 1978.

Bankston, Douglas. 'Wrap Shot', *American Cinematographer*, March 2000.

Barreca, Regina. 'David Lean's *Great Expectations*', in John Glavin (ed.) *Dickens on Screen*. Cambridge: Cambridge University Press, 2003.

Bourdieu, Pierre. *The Field of Cultural Production: Essays on Art and Literature*. Edited and introduced by Randal Johnson. Cambridge: Polity Press, 1993.

British Film Institute. Film and TV data base on line www.screenonline.org.uk/

Broadcast, 9 October 1998. (Based on interview with producer of 1999 TV version.)

Brownlow, Kevin. *David Lean*. London: Richard Cohen, 1996.

Chapman, James. *Past and Present: National Identity and the British Historical Film*. London: I.B. Tauris, 2005.

DeBona, Guerric. 'Doing Time; Undoing Time': 'Plot Mutation in David Lean's *Great Expectations*', both in *Literature/Film Quarterly*, Vol. 20, No. 1, 1991.

Durgnat, Raymond. *A Mirror for England*. London: Faber and Faber, 1970.

Anon. 'The musical that never was', *Films Illustrated*, Vol. 4, No. 38, October 1974.

Forster, John. *The Life of Dickens (1872–4)*. Rpt. London: J.M. Dent, 1966.

George, Thomas, R. *Dickens' 'Great Expectations'*. London: Edward Arnold, 1977.

Giddings, Robert. *Great Expectations* (the 1999 TV version), re-published from *The Dickensian*, on line at www.fidnet.com/

Guiliano, Edward & Collins, Philip (eds). *The Annotated Dickens. Volume 2*. New York: Clarkson N. Potter, Inc., 1986.

Guinness, Alec. *Blessings in Disguise* (1985). London: Fontana Paperbacks, 1986.

Hopkins, Charles. 'Great Expectations'. *Magill's Survey of Cinema – English Language Films*, First Series, Vol. 2, New Jersey: Salem Press, 1980, pp. 685–689.

House, Humphry. *The Dickens World*. London: Oxford University Press, 1976.

Johnson, Michael K. 'Not Telling the Story the Way It Happened: Alfonso Cuarón's *Great Expectations, Literature/Film Quarterly*, '. 33, No. 1.

Lambert, Gavin. 'British Films 1947: Survey and Prospect'. *Sequence 2*, Winter 1947, pp. 9–14.

Leavis, Q.D. 'How We Must Read *Great Expectations*'. In F.R. Leavis and Q.D. Leavis, *Dickens the Novelist*. Harmondsworth: Penguin 1972.

Lean, David. '*Brief Encounter*', in *Penguin Film Review*, No. 4. London and New York: Penguin, 1947.

Lejeune, C.A. 'Communiqués from the London film front', *New York Times*, 29 June 1947.

Lusted, David. 'Literary Adaptations and Cultural Fantasies', *Journal of Popular British Cinema*, No. 4, 2001.

McFarlane, Brian (ed.), *An Autobiography of British Cinema*. London: Methuen/BFI, 1977.

McFarlane, Brian. 'David Lean's *Great Expectations*: Meeting Two Challenges', *Literature/Film Quarterly*, Vol. 20, No. 1, 1992, pp. 70–73.

McFarlane, Brian. 'A Literary Cinema? British Films and British Novels', In Barr, Charles (ed.). *All Our Yesterdays: 90 Years of British Cinema*, London: BFI Publishing, 1986.

McFarlane, Brian. *Novel to Film: An Introduction to the Theory of Adaptation*. Oxford: Clarendon Press, 1996.

R.M. '*Great Expectations*', *Monthly Film Bulletin*, December 1946.

Magill, Frank N. (ed.). *Cinema: The Novel Into Film*. Pasadena: Salem Softbacks, 1980.

Maxford, Howard. '*Great Expectations*', *Film Review*, No. 604, April 2001.

Moynahan, Julian. 'Seeing the Book, Reading the Movie', in M. Klein and G. Parker (eds) *The English Novel and the Movies*. New York: Frederick Ungar Publishing Co., 1981.

Murphy, Robert. *Realism and Tinsel: Cinema and Society in Britain 1939–1948*. London: Routledge, 1989.

Nairne, Campbell (article reviewing four Dickens-based films of the 1930s). *Cinema Quarterly*, Spring 1935.

Page, Norman. *A Dickens Companion*. London and Basingstoke: Macmillan, 1984.

Page, Norman (ed.). *Hard Times, Great Expectations* and *Our Mutual Friend*: A Casebook. London and Basingstoke: Macmillan, 1979.

Powell, Dilys 'Films Since 1939', in *Since 1939*. London: Readers' Union and British Council, 1948.

Powell, Dilys. *Sunday Times*, December, 1946 (reprinted in George Perry (ed.), *The Golden Screen*. London: Pavilion Books, 1989, p. 63).

Pratley, Gerald. *The Cinema of David Lean*. London: Tantivy Press, 1974, pp. 58–71.

Propp, Vladimir. *Morphology of the Folktale* (1928), trans. Laurence Scott. Austin: University of Texas Press, 1968.

Reisz, Karel. *The Technique of Film Editing*. London: Focal Press, 1953.

Rosenberg, Edgar (ed.). *Great Expectations. A Norton Critical Edition*. London and New York: W.W. Norton & Company, 1999.

Sadrin, Anny. *Great Expectations*. London: Unwin Hyman, 1988.

Silver, Alain and Ursini, James. *David Lean and His Films*. Los Angeles: Silman-James Press, 1992.

Silverman, Stephen M. *David Lean*. London: André Deutsch, 1989.

Smith, Grahame. *Dickens and the Dream of Cinema*. Manchester: Manchester University Press, 2003.

Sloane, P.J 'The Sweetest Perfection', in *Film Review*, May 1998.

Vermilye, Jerry. *The Great British Films*. Secaucus, New Jersey: The Citadel Press, 1978.

Winnington, Richard. *Drawn and Quartered*. London: The Saturn Press. Date not given but c1948.

Winnington, Richard. 'Critical Survey'. *The Penguin Film Review 2*. Harmondsworth: London, 1947.

Wrathall, John. *'Great Expectations', Sight and Sound,* Vol. 8, No. 5, May 1998.

Zambrano, A.L. '*Great Expectations*: Dickens and David Lean' *Literature/Film Quarterly,* Vol. 2, No. 2, Spring 1974.

index

··